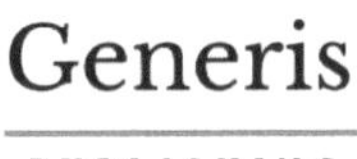

Generis
PUBLISHINC

AF406557

DESCRIEREA CIP A CAMEREI NAŢIONALE A CĂRŢII DIN REPUBLICA MOLDOVA

The effect of Kiambu County Government support initiatives on the growth of Micro Enterprises in Thika Sub-County, Kenya / Odhiambo Odera, Irene Kinyua, Florence Kaku, J. Kuria Thuo : Generis Publishing, 2020 (Print on demand). – 59 p. : fig. color, tab.

Referinţe bibliogr.: p. 48-56.

ISBN 978-9975-153-52-2.

334.72(676.2)

E 20

Cover image: www.pixabay.com

Generis Publishing
Online orders: www.generis-publishing.com
Orders by email: info@generis-publishing.com

Acknowledgements

We acknowledge the efforts of Prof. J. Kuria Thuo for initiating the Faculty Research Forums at Gretsa University from where the concept of this study emerged. We greatly appreciate the financial and material support from Gretsa University that funded the entire research project. Lastly, we are grateful to Mr. Samuel K. Muthondu, the Finance Officer of Kiambu County Government for the assistance he accorded us in obtaining the database of all registered micro enterprises in Thika Sub-County.

Table of Contents

Table of Contents.. 6

List of Tables.. 8

List of Figures 9

Definitions of Key Terms 10

List of Abbreviations and Acronyms.. 11

Executive Summary 13

Chapter One.. 1

   1.0 Introduction... 1

   1.1   Review of the Micro enterprises setup in Thika Sub-County 2

   1.2 Thika Sub-County Profile.. 3

   1.3 Problem Statement 4

   1.4 Objectives 5

   1.5 Hypothesis.. 5

   1.6 Conceptual Framework 7

Chapter Two 8

2.0 Theoretical Framework: Resource Based Theory 8

   2.1 Review of existing literature... 9

Chapter Three.. 13

   3.0 Research Design... 13

   3.1Target population 14

   3.2 Sampling Frame 14

   3.3 Sample distribution 15

   3.4 Research Instruments and Data Collection.. 15

   3.6 Data analysis 17

Chapter Four: Findings of the Study 18

   4.0 Introduction.. 18

   4.1 Response rate 18

   4.2 Firm Factors 18

      4.2.1 Gender of the Respondents.. 19

      4.2.2 Respondents Age Bracket 20

      4.2.3 Category of Business... 21

      4.2.4 How long has the Business been in Existence 23

      4.2.5 Position in the Business... 24

      4.2.6 Sources of Capital 25

      4.2.7 Level of Education 26

   4.3 Micro Enterprise Growth 27

4.3.1 Reliability and Factor Analysis..27

4.3.2 Normality Test for Growth...28

4.3.3 Firm's Profitability Performance 28

4.3.4 Firm's Sales..29

4.4 Policy Frameworks 30

4.4.1 Descriptive Statistics for Policy Frameworks..30

4.4.2 Correlation Analysis...31

4.4.3 Reliability Results for Policy Frameworks 31

4.5 Incentive programmes...31

4.5.1 Descriptive statistics for Incentive Programmes..32

4.5.2 Correlation Analysis...32

4.5.3 Reliability Results 33

4.6 Business Skills 33

4.6.1 Descriptive Statistics for Business Skills...33

4.6.2 Correlation Analysis for Business Skills and Micro Enterprises
Growth..34

4.6.3 Reliability Analysis 34

4.7 Hypothesis Testing 35

4.7.1 Hypothesis One 35

4.7.2 Hypothesis Two..37

4.7.3 Hypothesis Three..38

4.7.4 Hypothesis Four 39

4.7.5 Hypothesis Five..41

4.7.6 Hypothesis Six..42

Chapter Five: Summary of Findings, Conclusions and Recommendations....45

5.0 Summary of Findings..45

5.1 Conclusions...46

5.2 Recommendations...46

5.3 Suggestions for further research 47

References **48**

Appendix 1: Questionnaire...**57**

List of Tables

Table 1: Sample Distribution 15

Table 2: Gender of the Respondents 19

Table 3: Respondents Age bracket... 20

Table 4: Respondents Category of Business... 21

Table 5: Period of Business Existence 23

Table 6: Position in the Business 24

Table 7: Sources of Capital 25

Table 8: Level of Education 26

Table 9: Reliability 27

Table 10: Factor Analysis for Sales Turnover and Profitability 27

Table 11: Tests of Normality 28

Table 12: Firm's Profitability Performance 29

Table 13: Firm's Sales... 29

Table 14: Policy Frameworks 30

Table 15: Correlation between Policy Framework and Micro Enterprise Growth. 31

Table 16: Reliability Statistics for Policy Frameworks 31

Table 17: Descriptive statistics for Incentive Programmes 32

Table 18: Correlations between Incentives Programmes and Micro Enterprise Growth... 32

Table 19: Reliability Results for Incentive Programmes 33

Table 20: Descriptive Statistics for Business Skills... 33

Table 21: Correlations between Business Skills and Micro Enterprises Growth ... 34

Table 22: Reliability Statistics for Business Skills 34

Table 23: Model Summary... 35

Table 24: ANOVA[a] 36

Table 25: Coefficients[a] 36

Table 26: Model Summary... 37

Table 27: ANOVA[a] 37

Table 28: Coefficients[a] 38

Table 29: Model Summary... 38

Table 30: ANOVA[a] 39

Table 31: Coefficients[a] 39

Table 32: Model Summary... 40

Table 33: ANOVA[a] 40

Table 34: Coefficients[a] 40

Table 35: Model Summary... 41

Table 36: ANOVA[a] 42

Table 37: Coefficients[a] 42

Table 38: Model Summary 43

Table 39: ANOVA[a] 43

Table 40: Coefficients[a] 43

List of Figures

Figure 1. 1: Thika Sub County Wards Map 4
Figure 1. 2: Conceptual Framework 7
Figure 4. 1: Gender of the Respondents 19
Figure 4. 2: Age Bracket Distribution 20
Figure 4. 3: Category of Business 22
Figure 4. 4: Period of Business Existence 23
Figure 4. 5: Respondents Position in the Business 24
Figure 4. 6: Sources of Capital 25
Figure 4. 7: Level of Education 26
Figure 4. 8: Firm's Profitability Performance 29
Figure 4. 9: Firm's Sales 30

Definitions of Key Terms

Growth of micro enterprises: This is increase in size and profitability of the business.

Policy initiatives: These are initiatives to improve community life, solving serious problems of quality of life, social exclusion, and resource availability

Incentives programmes: These are formal scheme used to promote or encourage business owners to improve their business by increasing sales, attracting and retaining customers.

Business training: This is process of increasing the knowledge and skills on how to run the business.

List of Abbreviations and Acronyms

ANOVA: Analysis of Variance

GDP: Gross Domestic Product

GOK: Government of Kenya

SPSS: Statistical Package for Social Sciences

Executive Summary

Micro Enterprises are the major agents of economic growth and employment that lead to increased participation of the local people in the economy. The Government of Kenya has recognized the significance of micro enterprises development as a means of encouraging self-employment, poverty reduction and accelerating economic growth. As a result, the government has created a conducive business environment that ensures the expansion of the micro enterprise sector. By realizing the importance and potential of micro enterprises, governments in both developed and developing countries have initiated policies aimed at fostering their development by reducing problems facing the sector in financing, marketing, infrastructure and regulation. Micro enterprises have encountered many difficulties believed to have an impact on their growth. It is quite discouraging that the majority of micro enterprises continue to fail within a very short time and their unacceptable high failure rates are as a result of the numerous challenges they face. Problems associated with the growth of micro enterprises are diverse and they have faced numerous obstacles such as financial credit, viable market or inadequate support which highlight the challenges of the sector. The main objective of this study was to investigate the effects of Kiambu County Government support initiatives on the growth of micro enterprises in Thika sub-county. The specific objectives were: to determine the influence of policy initiatives on the growth of micro enterprises; to identify how incentives programmes affect micro enterprises growth and to assess how business skills affect micro enterprises growth. The study adopted a descriptive research design. The study targeted the 100 respondents working or owning the micro enterprises in 5 wards (Township ward, Hospital ward, Kamenu ward, Gatuanyaga ward and Ngoliba ward) in Thika Sub County. Primary data was obtained using self-administered questionnaires. Data was analysed using Statistical Package for Social Sciences (SPSS Version 25.0) which is the most recent version. Descriptive statistics such as frequencies, percentages, mean score and standard deviation was estimated for all the quantitative variables and information presented inform of tables. Inferential data analysis was done using regression and correlation analysis. The study concluded that Kiambu County Government policy frameworks affects micro enterprises growth. Although the initiatives have not led to reduced process of acquiring/ renewal of licenses and less business registration requirements. The study established that Kiambu County Government incentive programmes have a significant effect on micro enterprises growth in Thika Sub-County. The study established that Kiambu

County Government business skills training programmes do not influence micro enterprises growth since it is clear that training in accounting, financial and marketing skills and training in computer and internet skills might not improve the business growth. The study concluded that there micro enterprises firm factors are not related to support initiatives of Kiambu County Government, however they tend to affect the growth of micro enterprises in Thika Sub-County significantly. The Kiambu county government needs to come up with a supportive policy for the establishment of documentation centres and information networks to provide information to microenterprises entrepreneurs since most of the stakeholders of the micro enterprises seemed not to be aware on the importance of various county government initiatives. There is a need for the county government of Kiambu to come up with strategies to ensure that the owners and the stakeholders of the micro enterprises in Thika Sub County are aware of the need of having business skills and also conduct training for interested stakeholders at a reduced cost or no cost. This will improve their business skills and hence improve the performance of the business.

Chapter One

1.0 Introduction

Micro enterprises are a catalyst and key factor in the economies of many developing countries. The micro enterprise sector is one of the primary driving forces for job creation and poverty alleviation (Mutiria, 2017). Micro enterprises are increasingly recognized as important drivers of productivity and are widely accepted as a major aspect of economic dynamism (Hisrich, 2014). Visser (2013) argued that micro enterprises form the backbone of developing countries and are a main source of income for most people in urban and rural communities. In Sub-Saharan Africa, micro enterprises account for about 90% of all businesses and over 80% of new jobs that are created (Rambo, 2013). Thus, governments should provide increased resources to support micro enterprises due to their increasing importance.

A number of factors have contributed to the rapid expansion of micro enterprises which include retrenchment, downsizing and reduced employment opportunities in the formal sector. The rapid growth of micro enterprises indicated by profitability and sales turnover in any economy suggests a positive progress for any country (Mong'are, 2017). Studies have established that significant associations exist between profitability and sales turnover as predictors of business growth (Churchill & Lewis, 2013). The micro enterprises in South East Asian countries like China, Japan, India and Korea have grown in terms of profitability and sales turnover based on the production of quality goods and services (Maragia, 2013).

Micro enterprises tend to thrive in an environment that supports business growth, where the regulatory regime is transparent and decisions are made consistently that favors growth. One of the major challenges facing developing countries is the transformation of informal micro enterprises to the formal sector, to enable them enhance access to government support services (Mutiria, 2017). Some governments in developing countries in the past decades have placed emphasis on boosting their economic growth through the formulation of policies that support micro enterprises (Thuranira, 2017).The role of government is crucial in promoting and enhancing micro enterprises access to credit and education (Ackah &Vuvor, 2011). Berg et al. (2015) argues that governments perform a critical role in enlightening micro enterprises on types of funding options available, and awareness trainings on financial risk management.

Aremu & Adeyemi (2015) state that in Nigeria, despite government support through incentive programs, most micro enterprises in Nigeria still struggle to access credit or even attain enterprise growth. They argued that socio-economic obstacles within the business regulation systems affect micro enterprises growth. Lack of business experience, incoherent laws and regulations hinder the growth of micro enterprises. Government interventions through tax incentives and market creation have gone a long way in establishing a thriving business condition (Kimuyu, 2014).

While the contributions of micro enterprises to development are generally acknowledged, they have continually faced many obstacles such as financial credit, viable market or lack of support from the government. Iota & Wehinger (2015) identified various challenges faced by micro enterprises including inadequate education and skills, technological change, poor infrastructure, scanty market information and lack of access to credit. The challenge of poor working conditions, high taxation, and lack of business training continue to hinder the growth of micro enterprises in Kenya (Marlow, 2013). Poor government revenues, budgetary constraints and inadequate policies on micro enterprises have made it difficult for them to access financing (Obura & Matuvo, 2011).

Previous studies on micro enterprises in Kenya have focused on social, economic and administrative expertise that hinders the growth of micro enterprises. However, the proposed study will focus on factors that support the growth of micro enterprises at County Government level. The research will be conducted in Kiambu County, Thika sub-county which is one of the country's most prolific business towns in Kenya. Micro enterprises have been selected as they form a huge sector of Kenya's economy and present great potential in wealth creation and employment. Since micro enterprises dominate the business environment in Thika, a better understanding of this sector may help in facilitating its growth.

1.1   Review of the Micro enterprises setup in Thika Sub-County

Most micro enterprises fall under the informal sector and by extension, the term informal refers to people in self-employment or small-scale industries. Most micro enterprises in Thika Sub-County are replicative businesses which include small retail shops providing Mpesa and Mobile Phone accessories, Boda Boda and Tuk Tuk riders. Textile works such as tailoring, knitting and sewing of textile products are equally prevalent (Gathogo, 2011). Jua Kali sector where artisans make all types of merchandise from shoes, wheelbarrows, metal boxes and other assortment constitutes an integral part of the micro enterprises in Thika Sub-County. There are also woodworks businesses composing of furniture and carpentry. These micro enterprises are spread across Thika Sub-County especially in the densely populated areas like the Township, Makongeni, Kiganjo and Kianduttu.

There are a huge number of unemployed people due to redundancies, illiteracy and retrenchments among other factors. Some of the unemployed residents started their own small businesses in the hope of earning some kind of income. This led to the creation of more than over 2000 registered micro enterprises mainly drawn from the informal and Jua Kali sectors (GOK, 2006). The informal sector is estimated to constitute 98 percent of business in Kenya, contributing 30 percent of jobs and 3 percent of Kenya's GDP. The Kiambu County Government recognizes the role of the informal sector and seeks ways to integrate these businesses into the formal sector.

1.2 Thika Sub-County Profile

Thika Sub-County was selected because it is highly industrialized with a vibrant micro enterprises sector. It is an industrial town in Kiambu County, Kenya and is 42 kilometers north east of Nairobi, near the convergence of the Thika and Chania Rivers. Thika town is administratively in Kiambu County, and has a population of 139,853 which is rapidly growing. Thika is externally serviced by an eight-lane superhighway, a highway to Garissa and the rest of north-east Kenya, a highway to the central highlands and a railway line (with plans to add a passenger light rail to Nairobi). The Sub-County has a population of about 645,713 living in 171,569 households, making it the third most populous Sub-county in the County and eighth most populous nationally..

Figure 1. 1: Thika Sub County Wards Map

There are five wards in Thika Sub County as shown in Figure 1 above. These are Township, Hospital, Kamenu, Gatuanyaga and Ngoliba. The main economic activities include agricultural processing, particularly in horticulture and pineapple, coffee, cooking oils and animal feed processing. Other industries include textile, macadamia nuts, wheat, tannery, motor vehicle assemblies, cigarette manufacturing, bakeries, packaging and industrial chemicals. About 100 small-scale industries and about 20 major factories exist in and around the town. The service sector is well represented with the establishment and growth of a number of educational and financial institutions. Thika is home or close to three universities, tens of middle level colleges, hundreds of secondary and primary schools and dozens of financial institutions.

1.3 Problem Statement

Micro Enterprises are the major agents of economic growth and employment that lead to increased participation of the local people in the economy. The Government of Kenya has recognized the significance of micro enterprises development as a means of encouraging self-employment, poverty reduction and accelerating economic growth. As a result, the government has created a conducive business environment that ensures the expansion of the micro enterprise sector. By realizing the importance and potential of micro enterprises, governments in both developed and developing countries have initiated policies aimed at fostering their development by reducing problems facing the sector in financing, marketing, infrastructure and regulation.

Micro enterprises have encountered many difficulties believed to have an impact on their growth. It is quite discouraging that the majority of micro enterprises continue to fail within a very short time and their unacceptable high failure rates are as a result of the numerous challenges they face. Problems associated with the growth of micro enterprises are diverse and they have faced numerous obstacles such as financial credit, viable market or inadequate support which highlight the challenges of the sector. Lack of effective policy initiatives and incentives impede and undermine the growth of micro enterprises. Most micro enterprises have insufficient capacity in terms of skilled employees to manage their activities. Micro enterprises which lack government support policies have restricted access to improving their growth.

Despite their significances, a sizable number of micro enterprises fail within first few years of their business operations. Gichuki et al., (2014) indicate that three out of five micro enterprises fail within the first few months of operation and those that continue 80 per cent fail before the fifth year. Given this high failure rate, it becomes critical to research factors that can enable micro enterprises to survive. Many studies have been conducted on the factors influencing the growth of micro enterprises. However, these studies are done in different contexts and may not apply to the Kenyan micro enterprises context. This study therefore sought to investigate how Kiambu County Government supports the growth of micro enterprises in Thika Sub County.

1.4 Objectives

The main objective of this study was to investigate the effects of Kiambu County Government support initiatives on the growth of micro enterprises in Thika sub-county.

The specific objectives were:

1) To determine the influence of policy initiatives on the growth of micro enterprises.
2) To identify how incentives programmes affect micro enterprises growth.
3) To assess how business skills affect micro enterprises growth.

1.5 Hypothesis

H_o1: Kiambu County Government support initiatives have no effect on the growth of micro enterprises in Thika Sub-County.

H_o2: There is no relationship between Kiambu County Government policy frameworks and micro enterprises growth in Thika Sub-County.

H_o3: Kiambu County Government incentive programmes do not affect micro enterprises growth in Thika Sub-County.

H_o4: Kiambu County Government business skills training programmes do not influence micro enterprises Growth.

H_o5: There is no relationship between micro enterprises firm factors and the support initiatives of Kiambu County Government.

H_o6: Firm factors do not affect the growth of micro enterprises in Thika Sub-County.

1.6 Conceptual Framework

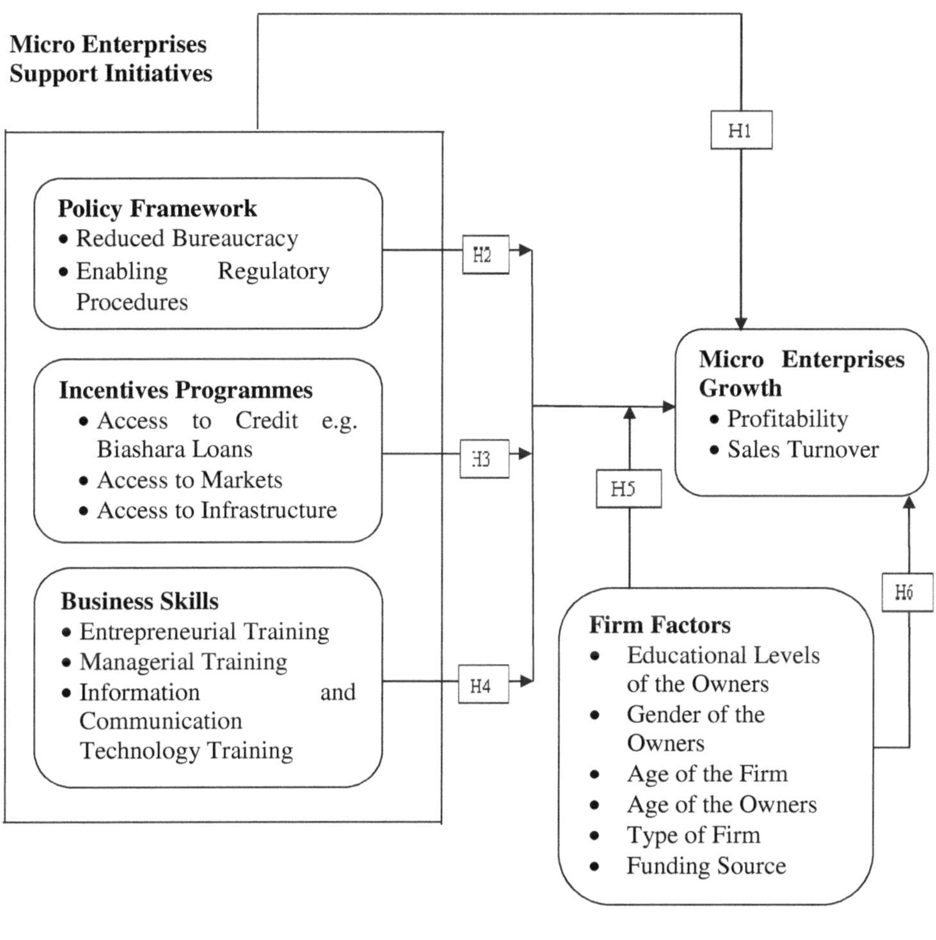

Figure 1. 2: Conceptual Framework

Chapter Two

2.0 Theoretical Framework: Resource Based Theory

The theoretical framework seeks to explain the relationship of variables and factors that affect growth of micro enterprises. The variables used to explain micro enterprises include the number of employees, annual sales turnover, assets, profitability, and these vary from industry to industry (Kushnir, 2010).According to the Resource Based Theory, availability of resources leads to sustained competitive advantage which in turn leads to growth of micro enterprises (Bunyasi, 2015). Resource Based Theory relates the role of a company's resources as the foundation for their strategy. The theory proposes that the resources and capabilities are a source of direction, and are the starting point of strategy formulation as they give a statement of the company's identity and purpose (Majama & Magang, 2017). Rindova & Fombrun (1999) argue that resources are essential for a company's competitive advantage. Wernerfelt (1984) asserts that a resource is anything which could be thought of as a strength or weakness of a given firm. Barney (1991) contends that such resources include all assets, capabilities, business processes, firm attributes, information, knowledge, etc. controlled by a company that enables micro enterprises to conceive of and implement strategies that improve their efficiency and effectiveness. Penrose (1959) suggested that a firm can be viewed as "a collection of productive resources"; and firms differ in fundamental ways as each has its own bundle of resources. Barney & Mackey (2005) state that resources have the potential to create economic value for the firms, if and only when companies realize and use the resources to create and implement strategic decisions.

The ability of micro enterprises to survive and grow depends on conditions of the external environment (Covin, 2014). In spite of their many contributions, micro enterprises are plagued by high failure rates and poor performance levels (Jocumsen, 2004). Resource availability is one of the areas where micro enterprises lack strength (Rahman, 2015). A frequent excuse for business failure is the actions of others: unfair laws and regulations, economic downturn, changes in customer tastes etc. (Gao, 2015). According to Mughan et al. (2004), one major reason for the failure of micro enterprises seems to be insufficient management capacity, lack of expertise, low levels of skills and managerial competences. One of the most important aspects of starting an micro enterprise or expanding an existing one is access to necessary resources (Watson, 2007).

Grant (1991) concludes the key of resource based theory is in understanding the relationship between resources, capabilities, competitive advantage and growth. The resource-based view predicts that certain types of resources owned and controlled by companies have the potential to generate superior performance (Ainuddin et al., 2007). This view focuses on a company's resources as a way to explain its growth. It rests on the assumption that a company's resources are influential in its achievement of growth (Davidsson & Wiklund, 1999). Therefore, resource based theory will be used to demonstrate that adequate resource support and policies to create capability are critical for micro enterprises growth as they are small in size and need assistance. Resource based theory will provide a framework to explain how business can identify suitable measures to overcome growth obstacles, have better access to manpower resources, financial resources, infrastructure, and access to the market (Nguyen et al., 2008).

2.1 Review of existing literature

The research field on micro enterprise growth has drawn considerable attention from both government and scholars alike (Gao, 2015). Sanjo & Ibrahim (2017) state that micro enterprises are generally privately owned organizations set-up for the purposes of producing goods or services for profit. The criteria for classifying business enterprises under micro enterprises differ from country to country (Aremu & Adeyemi, 2011; Nyagah, 2013). This has made it difficult to come out with a single universally accepted definition for micro enterprises. Ezeh (1999) suggested that the identifiable and predominant criteria across the globe for micro enterprises definition include: size of capital invested, number of staff or employees, size of turnover or sales volumes and value of assets. Based on the number of employees, a micro-enterprise is defined as having no more than 10 employees (Lois & Annette, 2005).

Governments all over the world have designed a number of support services for micro enterprises which include the policy initiatives for the purpose of creating and developing the micro enterprises sector (Mutiria, 2017). Many governmental bodies consider that the implementation of small businesses support will result in a stronger competitive position for the country (Chamanski & Waago, 2003). Chaston & Mangles (2002) argue that governments have paid increasing attention to the need to support micro enterprises development as a means of achieving their policy aims. Grimm & Paffhausen (2014) state that policy intervention focusing on improving the framework conditions for micro enterprises may entail labour market regulations and credit information systems. Ramsden (2010) asserts that micro enterprises thrive in environments that support business growth, where the regulatory regime is transparent and where physical infrastructure such as road and rail networks, power and telecommunications are adequate to facilitate trade. Support programs are designed to assist micro enterprises by linking them to the larger developmental vision of the nation with the main focus being poverty reduction and growth of small firms (Charbonneau & Menon, 2013).

Government policies and regulations on licensing/ permits, taxation and corruption affect the growth of micro enterprises to a great extent (Mugodo, 2014). According to Rambo (2013), the Kenyan government has put mechanisms in place such as the Micro and Small Enterprises Act as an initiative aimed at encouraging Kenyans in the micro enterprises sector to access financing. Similarly, Kiraithe (2015) notes that other Kenya Government national initiatives includes the establishment of Youth Entrepreneurship Development Fund (YEDF) aimed at empowering young entrepreneurs by providing an enabling environment. Additionally, the UWEZO fund initiative was meant to train micro enterprises, create market opportunities, facilitate supply chain linkages and provide infrastructural support for youth micro enterprises (Wanjohi, 2010).

Various studies have indicated that bureaucracy in the government in terms of business registration, issuing licenses and permits, tax payment etc. may create a strong regulatory barrier to micro enterprises growth (Bouazza et al., 2015; Mashenene & Rumanyika, 2014). Bureaucracy involves overly complicated regulation and wherever present, it slows down systems and operations (Nyarku & Oduro, 2017). Fiestas & Sinha (2011) stated that the paper work involved is mountainous and when correctly filled out and properly submitted with the requisite fees, getting the paper signed, stamped and approved becomes a monumental task. According to World Bank (2016), these bottlenecks in the public administrative systems reduce the entry and growth rate of micro enterprises. Hayford (2012) contends that bureaucracy affects the ability of micro enterprises to secure credit which slows the rate of micro enterprises growth.

Access to credit by micro enterprises is usually affected by lack of adequate collateral and information concerning entrepreneurs' credit worthiness constituting the major reasons of bank loan declines (Badulescu, 2011). Collateral has been one of the major stumbling blocks for micro enterprises seeking financing in their formative stages (Kiraithe, 2015). A study in Ghana revealed that lack of collateral, high cost of borrowing and absence of audited financial statement makes it difficult for micro enterprises to access bank loans (Ackah & Vuvor, 2011). Most micro enterprises, particularly in the startup stage lack the necessary relationship connections with banks, therefore decreasing the banks willingness to advance credit (Bonfim et al., 2012). As such, micro enterprises will continually have difficulties in accessing bank loans for the foreseeable future (Berg et al., 2015; Wangui et al., 2014). Access to micro enterprise financing is one of the most critical aspects of their survival and the lack of access to long term credit is a major challenge to those micro enterprises that would like to expand their operational activities (Wanjohi, 2010).Financial accessibility is instrumental to the development and growth of micro enterprises (Hallberg, 2014; Mead & Liedholm, 2013).

The complexity of the tax system raises the cost of doing business, as many micro enterprises do not have the capacity to administer tax returns and thus need to consult experts for a fee in order to meet these legal requirements (Luiz, 2011). Tomlin (2008) argued that small taxpayers within the taxation system usually suffer discrimination since compliance on tax issues are the same for both small and large companies (Gachuhi, 2016).Robertson et al. (2003) note that higher taxation rates on licenses for operating micro enterprises inhibits their development. Equally, Belliveau & Sandberg (2009), state that higher taxes raise the cost of doing business, making micro enterprises sustainability a volatile venture. Reducing the tax compliance costs for micro enterprises e.g. through the I-Tax, would increase the number of micro enterprises paying taxes and also have a positive outlook in their profit margins (Gachuhi, 2016). Government interventions through tax incentives for micro enterprises can establish a thriving business condition and environment.

According to King & McGrath (2010), there is a strong positive relationship between the level of education and growth of micro enterprises. Mugo (2014) investigated factors affecting women entrepreneurs' on the growth of their micro enterprises in Nairobi and revealed variables such as lack of entrepreneurial training and education as the key elements. Al-Madhoun & Analoui (2003) observed that owner managers resist advancing their management skills through training programs. Some were reluctant to hire qualified and skilled enterprise managers, which prevents the ability of micro enterprises to grow or even survive. Iota & Wehinger (2015) identified various challenges faced by micro enterprises including lack of innovative capacity, managerial training and experience. Berg et al. (2015) argues that governments performs a critical role in enlightening micro enterprises within local communities on types of funding options available and trainings on financial risk management.

Various studies have been conducted in Kenya based on the growth of micro enterprises. Yeboah (2015) notes that micro enterprises undergo seven stages of growth: product and service development, expansion, professionalism, consolidation of activities, diversification, integration, and decline and revitalization. Micro enterprise growth may be measured using growth indicators such as sales level, profit, asset turnover, employment and increase in physical output (Tundi & Tundi, 2012; Delmar et al., 2003). Wanjau et al. (2013) studied the role of quality on the growth of micro enterprises and explained that adoption of quality influences the growth of micro enterprises. Namusonge (2011) examined the elements of growth oriented micro enterprises and concluded that the availability and the type of finance are crucial elements that contribute to the growth of micro enterprises. Previous studies on micro enterprises development in Kenya largely focused on social, economic and administrative expertise that hinders the growth of the micro enterprises (Obura & Matuvo, 2011; Mira & Ogollah, 2013; Kiraithe, 2015). Few studies have focused on the role of Kiambu County Government in supporting the growth of micro enterprises in Thika Sub-County, Kenya and this study seeks to fill this gap.

Chapter Three

3.0 Research Design

A research design provides a study framework for streamlining the scope of and mechanics through which the study objectives can be achieved (Mugenda & Mugenda, 2012). The research adopted a cross sectional descriptive survey design. The mixed method approach was used where both quantitative and qualitative approaches were adopted with the aim of determining the relationship between County Government support and the growth of micro enterprises. According to Johnson et al. (2007), mixed methods is where a study mixes or combines both quantitative and qualitative research techniques, methods, approaches concepts or language into a single study.

Descriptive research design was used in order to describe the County Government factors influencing the growth of micro enterprises and examine the relationship between the dependent and independent variables. Descriptive research obtains information that concerns the current status of phenomena and describes what exists with respect to variables or conditions in a particular situation (Creswell, 2014).This study adopted a cross-sectional research design as it allowed the comparison of the extent to which at least two sectors of micro enterprises differed on the dependent variables (Bryman & Bell, 2007). This research design was suitable because of the need to identify and describe factors that influence the growth of micro enterprises and to gain an understanding of the relationship between dependent and independent variables that was being studied (Mong'are, 2017).

Quantitative analysis was adopted with numerical values to establish the relationship between the dependent and independent variables using a structured survey questionnaire. Qualitative analysis was used to determine from the owners and managers of micro enterprises which types of factors they thought greatly influenced the growth of their businesses. Regression and correlation analysis was used to generate inferential statics for prediction purposes (Sekaran, 2006).A survey of the micro enterprises in Thika Sub-County was conducted where the list of registered micro enterprises was obtained from the current registration documents of Kiambu County Government as at end of 2018.

3.1Target population

Sekaran & Bougie (2013) describe a population as the entire group of people, events or things of interest that a researcher wishes to investigate. Similarly, a population refers to an entire group of objects or events having common characteristics for observation, the aggregate of what conforms to certain specifications (Mugenda & Mugenda, 2012).The study targeted the owners and managers of micro enterprises that have been in operation for more than one year at the time of the study. The target population for this study comprised of all licensed micro enterprises in Jua Kali sector, retail shops, general trade, Boda Boda/Tuk Tuk, textile works and hospitality sector.

The study targeted the 4805 persons working or owning the micro enterprises in 5 wards (Township ward, Hospital ward, Kamenu ward and Ngoliba ward, Gatuanyaga ward) in Thika Sub County

3.2 Sampling Frame

A sampling technique is defined as the method that a researcher employs to pick a sample size from the entire population (Cooper & Schindler, 2014). Stratified random sampling technique was adopted in this study which included different sectors within micro enterprises. The micro enterprises were first stratified according to the nature of their businesses and then samples were then selected from each stratum using stratified random sampling. This enabled the capture of all sectors of micro enterprises in Thika Sub-County. Within each strata or trade area, the owners or managers were picked using stratified random sampling.

A sample size is defined as the element of a study that represents the actual population, or that elements to be examined within a study, from which, inference will be made to the entire population (Babbie, 2010). The study adopted convenience sampling to select an appropriate sample size from the population (Nyagah, 2013). A sample of 100 was selected as the representative sample size from the owners or managers of micro enterprises operating within Thika Sub-County.

3.3 Sample distribution

The sample of 100 respondents was distributed as illustrated in Table 1.

Table 1: Sample Distribution

Ward	Sample	Percent
Township ward	20	20%
Hospital ward	20	20%
Kamenu ward	20	20%
Gatuanyaga ward	20	20%
Ngoliba ward	20	20%
Total	**100**	**100**

3.4 Research Instruments and Data Collection

The study adopted two main methods of collecting data i.e. primary and secondary methods. The key instruments used were the self-administered questionnaire designed for the owners and managers of the micro enterprises. Primary data was collected using a structured questionnaire with fixed set of choices closed questions. Cooper & Schindler (2014) advocates for the use questionnaires in descriptive studies because it is less costly and participants can easily be reached. Questionnaires increased the rate of response and helped the researcher accumulate and summarize responses easily (Kothari, 2009, William, 2006). Secondary data was obtained from historical documents such as official publications of the Kiambu County Government which listed all registered micro enterprises in the County. Secondary data involves information not collected directly but is from published materials and other sources. It is easily available, convenient and cost effective (Kombo & Tromp, 2006).

3.5 Measurement of Variables

Variable	Measure Construct	Indicator	Question Number
Policy Frameworks	Reduced Bureaucracy	Process of acquiring/ renewal of licenses	10
	Enabling Regulatory Procedures	Business registration requirements	11
Incentives Programmes	Access to Credit	Business Loans	12
	Access to Markets	Preference in purchases	13
	Access to Infrastructure	Roads, Water, Sewage and Sanitation	14
Business Skills	Entrepreneurial Training	Business Knowledge and Practices	15
	Managerial Training	Accounting, Financial and Marketing Skills	16
	Information and Communication Technology Training	Computer and Internet Skills	17
Firm Factors	Educational levels of the Owners	Formal Qualifications	7
	Gender of the Owners	Male/Female	1
	Age of the Firm	Years	4
	Age of the Owners	Years	2
	Type of Firm	Category of Business	3
	Funding Source	Sources of Capital	6
MEs Growth	Profitability	Profit Margin	8
	Sales Turnover	Inventory sold & replaced	9

3.6 Data analysis

Data was analysed using Statistical Package for Social Sciences (SPSS Version 25.0) which is the most recent version. Descriptive statistics such as frequencies, percentages, mean score and standard deviation was estimated for all the quantitative variables and information presented inform of tables. Inferential data analysis was done using regression and correlation analysis. The regression analysis was used to establish the relations between the independent and dependent variables. Regressions were used because the procedure uses two or more independent variables to predict a dependent variable.

Chapter Four: Findings of the Study

4.0 Introduction

The chapter presents the empirical findings and results of the application of the variables using the techniques mentioned in chapter three. The study sought to examine the effect of Kiambu County Government support initiatives on the growth of micro enterprises in Thika sub-county, Kenya. The specific variables of the study were policy frameworks, incentive programmes and business skills. The intervening variable was the moderating effect of firm factors on the growth of micro enterprises in Thika sub-county. Specifically, the data analysis was in line with specific objectives where patterns were investigated, interpreted and implications drawn on them.

4.1 Response rate

The study sought to find the overall percentage of respondents who participated in the study. The percentage of people who respond to a survey is considered as the response rate. In general, response rate is the number of actual respondents or participants divided by the total number of targeted participants as per the sample size (Draugalis et al., 2008).Sampling was done based on convenience stratified sampling methods. The sampling method was used with the aim of ensuring inclusivity of all the different sub-sectors in the micro enterprise sector to ensure that the obtained results would be as representative as possible (Kang'ethe, 2018). Data was collected by the researchers visiting the targeted micro enterprise firms and interviewing either the business owners, managers or employees. There were 100 questionnaires which were self-administered by the researchers during the study. The response rate realized was 100% which amounted to a total of 100 micro enterprises. Orodho (2005) considered that at least 100 respondents was a good representation for a study.

4.2 Firm Factors

The study sought to establish the effect of firm factors on the growth of micro enterprises in Thika Sub County. These include Gender, Age bracket, categories of respondents business, period in which the respondents business have been in existence, respondents position in the business, Sources of capital and respondents level of education. The findings for the firm factors are presented in various sub sections.

4.2.1 Gender of the Respondents

The study sought to establish the Gender of the respondents as shown in Table 2 and Figure 2.

Table 2: Gender of the Respondents

	Frequency	Percent
Female	51	51
Male	49	49
Total	**100**	**100**

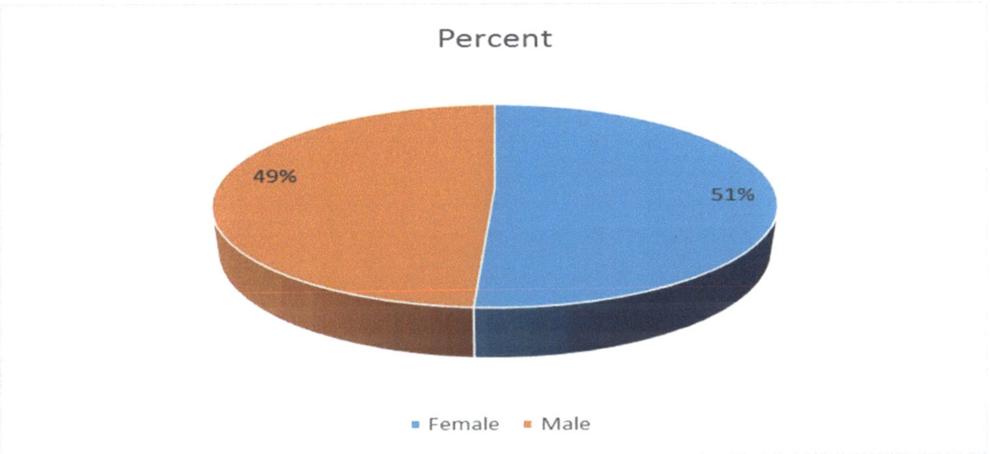

Figure 4. 1: Gender of the Respondents

From the findings, most of the respondents were female as shown 51% while the rest were male as shown by 49%. This is an indication that the study was not gender biased as data was collected from both genders. The results indicate that the two genders were adequately represented in the study since there is none which was more than the two-thirds. The study findings concur with Kimuru (2018) who revealed that the female gender could be dominating the micro enterprises sector in Thika sub-county. This could be attributed to the financial support to women through various schemes such as the Women Enterprise Funds (WEF) hence empowering more women to engage in more entrepreneurial activities (Kimuru, 2018). As such, the percentages indicate an increase in the number of women engaging in entrepreneurial activities. Similarly, Kyalo (2016) suggests that women are active participants in economic development through enterprise creation and development. The findings however negate those of Kangethe (2018) who found that the larger percentage of the respondents in manufacturing micro enterprises in Kenya were males comprising of 75% of the respondents. Ouma (2018) and Munyao (2018) indicated that most businesses were patriarchy but observed that more women were making good efforts in businesses. The findings show that majority of micro enterprises in Thika Sub-County are owned by, managed by or employs mainly female. This finding suggests that women were active participants in economic development through enterprise creation and development.

4.2.2 Respondents Age Bracket

The study findings for age bracket to which the respondents belong to were presented in Table 3 and Figure 3.

Table 3: Respondents Age bracket

	Frequency	Percent
18-30 years	30	30
31-40 years	38	38
41-50 years	18	18
Over 50years	14	14
Total	**100**	**100**

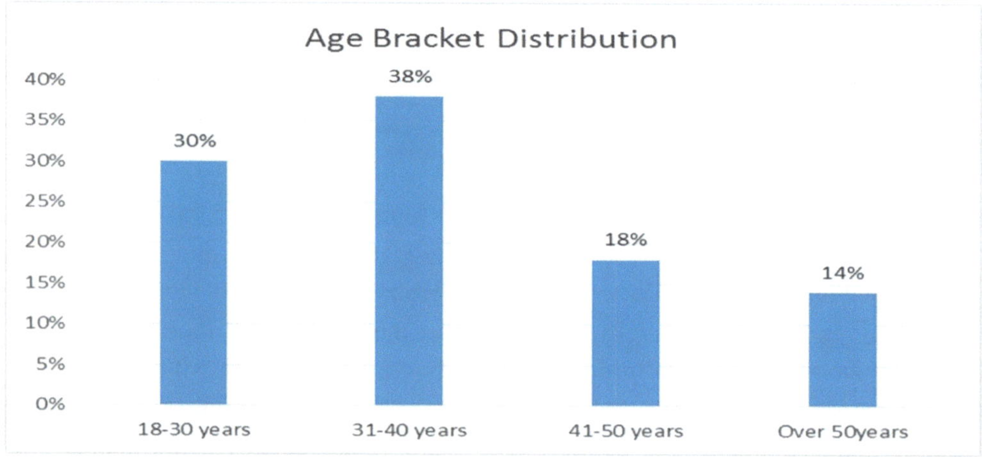

Figure 4. 2: Age Bracket Distribution

Age as a personal characteristic is a key factor in micro enterprise management. From the findings in Table 3 and Figure 3, the study recorded highest numbers of business owners and or managers in the age bracket between31 and 40 years as shown by 38%. This can be explained by the fact that at this age most people may have started working early and may have made some savings to enable them access more finances and start their own businesses (Bunyasi, 2015). Other respondents indicated to be aged between 18 and 30 years as shown by 30%, between 41 and 50 years as shown by 18% and over 50years as shown by 14%.

Most micro enterprises are owned and mainly run by people in their 30s which comprise of the youthful population. Parker (2004) argued that an individual's decision to start a business is influenced by their age and by the age distribution in the region where the individual lives. Ramadhan (2019) asserts that the rationale of positive impact of age on self-employment is based on the view that the quantity of the financial and human capital that one possesses and that are necessary for starting and conducting the business increases with age. Kyalo (2016) suggested that the prime age for entrepreneurial activity was between 30-40 years. These findings further concur with those of Nabutola, (2015) and Owino (2017) who explained that the younger owner/manager have the necessary motivation, energy and commitment to work and is more inclined to take risks.

4.2.3 Category of Business

The findings for respondents category of business was as shown in Table 4 and Figure 4.

Table 4: Respondents Category of Business

	Frequency	Percent
Jua Kali Sector	3	3
Retail Shops	59	59
General Trade	11	11
Textile Works	4	4
Hospitality Sector	9	9
Sub Total	86	86
Others	14	14
Total	**100**	**100**

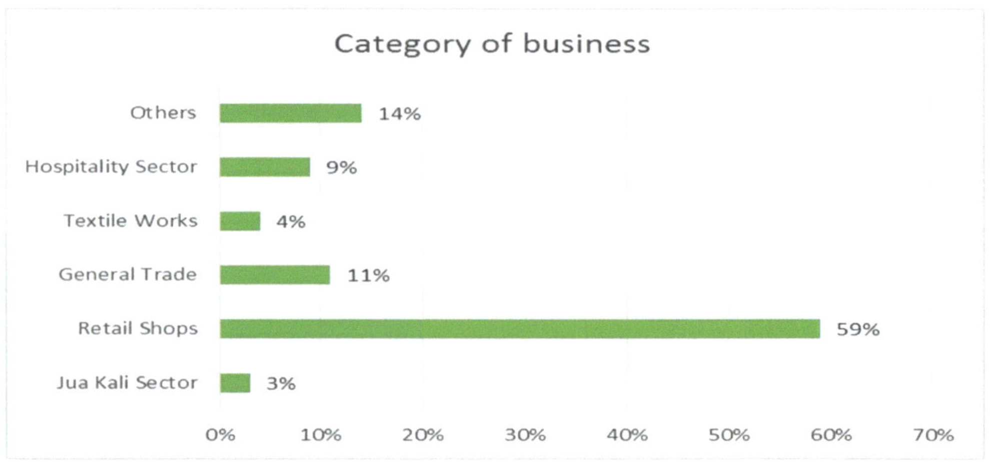

Figure 4. 3: Category of Business

From the findings, most respondents indicated that their business belonged to Retail Shops as illustrated by 59%. This can be attributed to the fact that Retail Shops needs lower startup costs than other specialized categories thereby making entry into the business easy for many. This is followed by General Trade as shown by 11% which do not require micro enterprise owners to possess specialized skills and high capital hence a slightly bigger percentage. The third category is the Hospitality Sector indicated by 9%, Textile Works illustrated by 4% and Jua Kali Sector as shown by 3%. Moreover, 14% of the respondents indicated that their business belong to other categories including Shoe Selling, Hardware, Agrovet, Cosmetics, School Uniforms, Financial Agencies, Chemist, Cyber Café, Salon, Beauty Parlour, Kinyozi, Auto Spares, Service Laundry, Photo Copy and Printing, Furniture Shop and Electronics.

The results imply that most the sectors were represented in the study thus giving an opportunity for the study to obtain diverse views and opinions on the study questions (Ramadhan, 2019).The findings concur with those by Madatta (2011) who revealed that most of the micro enterprises
Ilala and Temeke Municipals in Tanzania are based on trading sector which is easier to start and have a wider market but also require minimal qualifications. The trade sector accommodates diverse generalized skills and a relatively lower initial investment capital as compared to manufacturing and service departments thereby reducing barriers to entry (Moore et al., 2008).

4.2.4 How long has the Business been in Existence

The findings for the period in which the respondents business have been in existence were presented in Table 5 and Figure 5.

Table 5: Period of Business Existence

	Frequency	Percent
1-3 years	40	40
3-6 years	27	27
6-8years	8	8
8-10years	6	6
More than 10 years	19	19
Total	**100**	**100**

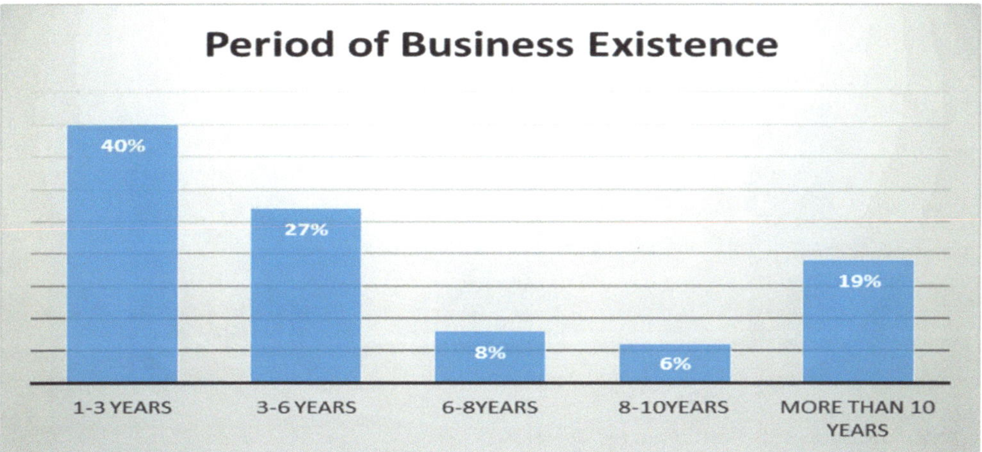

Figure 4. 4: Period of Business Existence

As per the findings, most of the businesses have been in existence for a period of 1-3 years as shown by 40%. This showed that most the enterprises were young and therefore, the entrepreneurial leadership may not have had the required work experience to spur them to high growth rates (Nyang'au, 2014).

Others business as indicated by the respondent had been existing for a period of 3-6 years as shown by 27%, more than 10 years as shown by 19%, 6-8years as shown by 8% and 8-10years as shown by 6%. The results contradict those of Bunyasi (2015) who found that majority of the micro enterprises in Thika have been in existence for over 10 years and have therefore grown over time by adopting the critical factors of human capital, access to finance and access to business information among others.

4.2.5 Position in the Business

The study sought to establish the respondent's position in the business which are presented in Table 6 and Figure 6.

Table 6: Position in the Business

	Frequency	Percent
Owner	50	50
Manager	18	18
Employee	32	32
Total	**100**	**100**

Figure 4. 5: Respondents Position in the Business

From the findings, majority of the respondents were the business owners as shown by 50% while other respondents were managers as shown by 18% and employees as shown by 32%.This is supported by Sitharam & Hoque (2016)who found that most of the respondents (69%)were the micro enterprise owners or both the manager and owner. This is reflective of the fact that many micro enterprise owners perform many roles. Nganu (2018) observed that the majority of the respondents in their study were owners of their micro enterprises businesses. This is reflective of the nature of the micro enterprises, which are mainly run by owner-managers. The results indicate that the study covered all designations in the management and operations of micro enterprises hence the information from the respondents was vital for the research. However, majority of the micro enterprises were operated by the owners as shown in the figure above.

4.2.6 Sources of Capital

The findings for the sources of capital of the respondents were presented in Table 7 and Figure 7.

Table 7: Sources of Capital

	Frequency	Percent
Personal & Family	81	81%
Others	19	19%
Total	**100**	**100**

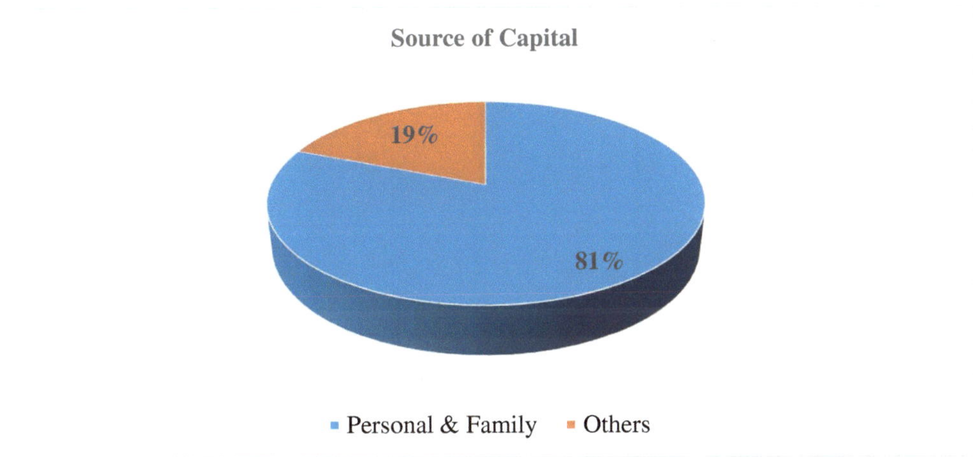

Figure 4. 6: Sources of Capital

From the findings in Table 7 and Figure 7, most of the respondents indicated that the source of their income was from personal savings and family as shown by 81% and other sources of income as shown by 19%.According to Ewiwile et al. (2012), sources of capital for micro enterprises includes; owner's savings, friends, family members, Banks, members of the trade, partners and shareholders. Njuguna (2016)revealed that the highest number of micro enterprises in Kariobangi area of Nairobi was funded and operated through the use of personal savings while the least had been started by money from friends.

The results concur with those of Kamunge et al. (2014) who established that majority (75.2%) of micro enterprises in Limuru Town Market obtained their initial capital from personal savings followed by 11.8% of the respondents who obtained their initial capital from family members. Similarly, Mutoko &

Kapunda (2017) found that the majority of manufacturing micro enterprises in Botswana use their own money (79.0%) to start and run their business.

4.2.7 Level of Education

The findings for the respondents level of education was as presented in Table 8 and Figure 8.

Table 8: Level of Education

	Frequency	Percent
University	22	22
College	40	40
Secondary	30	30
Primary	1	1
None	7	7
Total	**100**	**100**

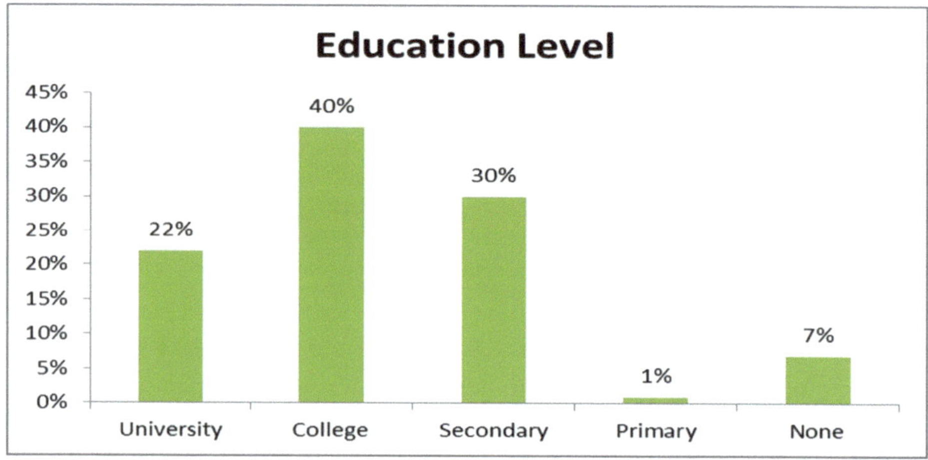

Figure 4. 7: Level of Education

The study sought to find out the respondents' distribution with respect their education background. Education is a crucial factor in the management of any business. Well educated entrepreneurs tend to manage their enterprises fairly in a sustainable manner and are able to coordinate management principles in the day to day operation of the businesses they run. In addition, educated entrepreneurs are better risk takers since they are able to predict situations beforehand and rightfully condition their enterprises in coping with them such that the economic effects are manageable (Kagika, 2016).

From the findings, most of the respondents indicated their highest level of education as college as shown by 40%. Other respondents indicated to have secondary as shown by 30% and university as shown by 22% as their highest level of education. Those who had no education were 7% and primary was only 1%. The study found that most of the respondents had a good educational background to manage the micro enterprises.

According to Nyang'au (2014), one might expect higher levels of formal education to spur micro enterprise growth by enhancing firm capabilities. For example, formal education may provide entrepreneurs with a greater capacity to learn about new production processes and product designs, offer specific technical knowledge conducive to firm expansion, and increase owners' flexibility. This is supported by Bunyasi (2015) who found 42% of the respondents had tertiary level education. However, the results contradict the argument by Ardic at al. (2011) that many micro enterprises are owned by individuals with minimal education background based on the fact that many of them do not land into the job markets thus create their own businesses.

4.3 Micro Enterprise Growth

The study sought to establish the growth trend of the Micro Enterprise in Thika Sub County. The findings were as follows.

4.3.1 Reliability and Factor Analysis

The findings for reliability and factor analysis were as presented in Table 9 and Table 10

Table 9: Reliability

	Cronbach's Alpha	N of Items
Micro Enterprise Growth	.939	2

From the findings, the Micro Enterprise Growth was found to be reliable as its Cronbach's Alpha (0.939) was greater than the threshold of 0.7.

Table 10: Factor Analysis for Sales Turnover and Profitability

	Component
	1

How would you rate your firm's profitability performance within the last three years of operation?	.971
How have your firm's sales faired in the last three years of operation?	.971
Extraction Method: Principal Component Analysis.	
a. 1 Components extracted.	

From the findings in Table 10, all the two items of Micro enterprise growth were pace under the same component. Its coefficients were greater than 0.4 hence the items needed no amendments.

4.3.2 Normality Test for Growth

The normality test was conducted using Kolmogorov-Smirnov coefficients.

Table 11: Tests of Normality

	Kolmogorov-Smirnov[a]		
	Statistic	**Df**	**Sig.**
Micro Enterprise Growth	.233	100	.000

From the findings, the Kolmogorov-Smirnov statistic was 0.233 and sig value was 0.00. This implies that the null hypothesis that Micro Enterprise Growth was not normally distributed was rejected and concluded that Growth of Micro Enterprise was normally distributed.

4.3.3 Firm's Profitability Performance

The respondents were requested to rate their firm's profitability performance within the last three years of operation. The findings were as presented in Table 12.

Table 12: Firm's Profitability Performance

	Frequency	Percent
Increased	38	38
No Change	26	26
Decreased	36	36
Total	**100**	**100**

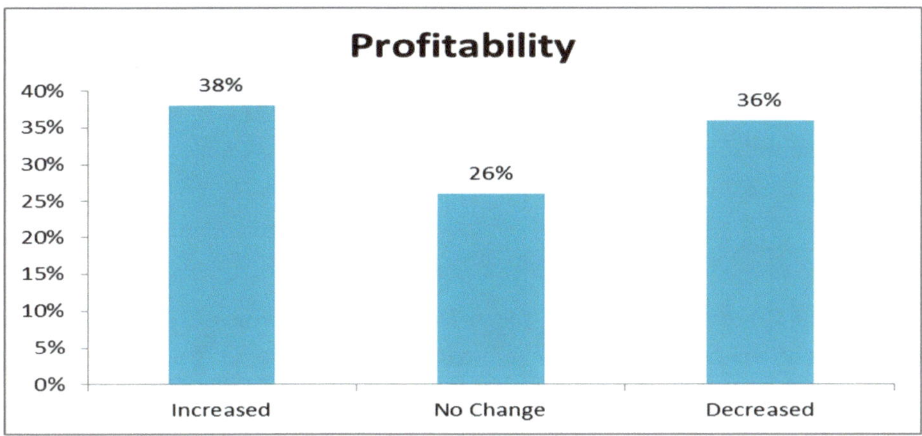

Figure 4. 8: Firm's Profitability Performance

From the findings, most of the respondents indicated that their business profitability have been increasing for the last three years as shown by 38%. Others indicated that their business have had decreasing profits for the last three years as shown by36% and others indicated constant profits for the last 3 years.

4.3.4 Firm's Sales

The respondents were requested to rate their firm's sales faired in the last three years of operation. The findings were as presented in Table 13.

Table 13: Firm's Sales

	Frequency	Percent
Increased	36	36
No Change	27	27
Decreased	37	37
Total	**100**	**100**

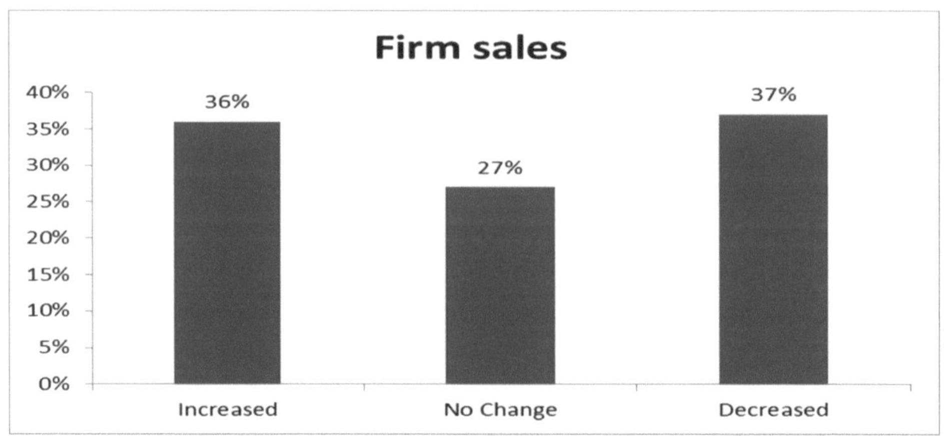

Figure 4. 9: Firm's Sales

The findings in Table 13 show that the sales of most businesses have been decreasing as shown by 37%. Other indicated an increase in sales in their business for the last 3 years as shown by 36% and constant sales for the last 3 years was indicated by 275.

4.4 Policy Frameworks

The study sought to determine the influence of policy initiatives on the growth of micro enterprises in Thika Sub County.

4.4.1 Descriptive Statistics for Policy Frameworks

The respondents were therefore asked to indicate their level of agreement with various statements on policy frameworks and the findings were shown in Table 14.

Table 14: Policy Frameworks

	Mean	Std. Dev.
Reduced process of acquiring/ renewal of licenses	3.210	1.458
Less business registration requirements	3.020	1.378

From the findings, the respondents neither agreed nor disagreed with statements that there is reduced process of acquiring/ renewal of licenses as shown by a mean of 3.21 and that there is less business registration requirements as shown by a mean of 3.0200.

4.4.2 Correlation Analysis

The study conducted a correlation analysis to assess the strength of relationship between the policy framework and micro enterprise growth and the findings were shown inn Table 15.

Table 15: Correlation between Policy Framework and Micro Enterprise Growth

		Microenterprise Growth	Policy Framework
Microenterprise Growth	Pearson Correlation	1	.031
	Sig. (2-tailed)		.762
	N	100	100
Policy Framework	Pearson Correlation	.031	1
	Sig. (2-tailed)	.762	
	N	100	100

The findings showed a weak correlation between policy framework and micro enterprise growth as shown by a correlation coefficient of 0.031.

4.4.3 Reliability Results for Policy Frameworks

The findings for reliability for policy frameworks were as presented in Table16.

Table 16: Reliability Statistics for Policy Frameworks

	Cronbach's Alpha	N of Items
Policy Frameworks	.817	2

From the findings the Cronbach's Alpha for Policy Frameworks was 0.817. This meant that the variable was reliable as its coefficient was greater than 0.7 threshold.

4.5 Incentive programmes

The study sought to identify how incentives programmes affect micro enterprises growth in Thika Sub County.

4.5.1 Descriptive statistics for Incentive Programmes

The respondents were also requested to indicate their level of agreement with various statements on incentives programmes and the findings were shown in Table 17.

Table 17: Descriptive statistics for Incentive Programmes

	Mean	Std. Dev.
Availability of Business Loans	2.540	1.344
Preference in purchases	2.500	1.291
Availability of roads, Water, Sewage and Sanitation	2.820	1.395

As per the findings, the respondents neither agreed nor disagreed on availability of roads, water, sewage and sanitation as shown by a mean of 2.8200, availability of business loans as shown by a mean of 2.5400 and on preference in purchases as shown by a mean of 2.5000.

4.5.2 Correlation Analysis

The study conducted a correlation analysis to assess the strength of relationship between the incentives programmes and micro enterprise growth and the findings were shown inn Table 15.

Table 18: Correlations between Incentives Programmes and Micro Enterprise Growth

		Microenterprise Growth	Incentive Programmes
Microenterprise Growth	Pearson Correlation	1	-.223[*]
	Sig. (2-tailed)		.025
	N	100	100
Incentive Programmes	Pearson Correlation	-.223[*]	1
	Sig. (2-tailed)	.025	
	N	100	100
*. Correlation is significant at the 0.05 level (2-tailed).			

Based on findings in Table 18, the study established a negative but significant relationship between Incentive Programmes and micro enterprise growth as shown by r=-0.223 and p=0.025.

4.5.3 Reliability Results

The findings for reliability for incentive programmes were as presented in Table19.

Table 19: Reliability Results for Incentive Programmes

	Cronbach's Alpha	N of Items
Incentive Programmes	.530	3

From the findings the Cronbach's Alpha for incentive programmes was 0.817. This meant that the variable was not reliable as its coefficient was less than 0.7 threshold and hence its items required amendments.

4.6 Business Skills

The study further sought to assess how business skills affect micro enterprises growth in Thika Sub County.

4.6.1 Descriptive Statistics for Business Skills

The respondents were requested to indicate their level of agreement with various statements on business skills and the findings were shown in Table 20.

Table 20: Descriptive Statistics for Business Skills

	Mean	Std. Dev.
Training in Business Knowledge and Practices	2.130	1.461
Training in Accounting, Financial and Marketing Skills	1.990	1.382
Training in Computer and Internet Skills	1.910	1.280

From the findings, the respondents neither agreed nor disagreed on training in business knowledge and practices as shown by a mean of 2.130. The respondents however disagreed on training in accounting, financial and marketing skills as shown by a mean of 1.990 and on training in computer and internet skills as shown by a mean of 1.910.

4.6.2 Correlation Analysis for Business Skills and Micro Enterprises Growth

The study conducted a correlation analysis to assess the strength of relationship between the business skills and micro enterprises growth and the findings were shown inn Table 21.

Table 21: Correlations between Business Skills and Micro Enterprises Growth

		Microenterprise Growth	Business Skills
Microenterprise Growth	Pearson Correlation	1	-.127
	Sig. (2-tailed)		.206
	N	100	100
Business Skills	Pearson Correlation	-.127	1
	Sig. (2-tailed)	.206	
	N	100	100

As per the findings in Table 21, the study established a negative and insignificant relationship between business skills and micro enterprise growth as shown by r= -0.127 and p=0.206.

4.6.3 Reliability Analysis
The findings for reliability for business skills were as presented in Table 9 and Table 10

Table 22: Reliability Statistics for Business Skills

	Cronbach's Alpha	N of Items
Business skills	.935	3

As per the findings, the Cronbach's Alpha for business skills was 0.935. This meant that the variable was reliable as its coefficient was greater than 0.7 threshold.

4.7 Hypothesis Testing

The study utilized regression analysis to test for the study hypotheses. The findings were presented in various subsections.

4.7.1 Hypothesis One

To test the first hypothesis that "Kiambu County Government support initiatives have no effect on the growth of micro enterprises in Thika Sub-County", the study conducted a regression analysis. The model that was used to test the hypotheses:

$$Y = a + \beta_1 X_1 + \beta_2 X_2 + \beta_3 X_3 + e$$

Y = Growth of micro enterprises in Thika Sub-County

a = Constant; B_1, B_2 and B_3 = Beta coefficients

X_1 = Policy frameworks

X_2 = Incentive programmes

X_3 = Business skills

e = error term

Table 23: Model Summary

Model	R	R Square	Adjusted R Square	Std. Error of the Estimate
1	.238[a]	.056	.027	1.65000
a. Predictors: (Constant), Business Skills, Policy Framework, Incentive Programmes				

The findings in Table 23, shows that R-Square value was 0.056, which indicates that the independent variables (business skills, policy framework and incentive programmes) explain 5.6% of the variation in the Growth of Micro Enterprise in Thika sub county.

Table 24: ANOVA[a]

Model		Sum of Squares	df	Mean Square	F	Sig.
1	Regression	15.629	3	5.210	1.914	.133[b]
	Residual	261.361	96	2.723		
	Total	**276.990**	**99**			
a. Dependent Variable: Micro Enterprise Growth						
b. Predictors: (Constant), Business Skills, Policy Framework, Incentive Programmes						

From the Anova Table, the finding shows that the F calculated was 1.914 and sig. value was 0.133. This shows that the overall model was insignificant since F calculated (1.914) was less than F critical (2.699) and sig value (0.133) was greater than 0.05.

Table 25: Coefficients[a]

Model		Unstandardized Coefficients		Standardized Coefficients	t	Sig.
		B	Std. Error	Beta		
1	(Constant)	4.727	.588		8.037	.000
	Policy Framework	.057	.070	.089	.813	.418
	Incentive Programmes	-.126	.070	-.217	-1.799	.075
	Business Skills	-.017	.056	-.040	-.311	.757
a. Dependent Variable: Micro Enterprise Growth						

From the findings the regression equation was

$$Y = 4.727 + 0.057X_1 - 0.126X_2 - 0.017X_3$$

The finding shows that holding other factors constant, the growth of micro enterprises had a coefficient of 4.727. Further, the study established that holding other factors constant, Policy Framework would lead to 0.057 insignificant change in growth of micro enterprises in Thika Sub County. In addition, Incentive Programmes would lead to negative 0.126 change in growth of micro enterprises in Thika Sub County and Business Skills would lead to negative 0.017 change in growth of micro enterprises in Thika Sub County. Based on the above findings, the null hypothesis was therefore accepted and it was concluded that Kiambu County Government support initiatives have no effect on the growth of micro enterprises in Thika Sub-County.

4.7.2 Hypothesis Two

To test the second hypothesis that "There is no relationship between Kiambu County Government policy frameworks and micro enterprises growth in Thika Sub-County", the study conducted a regression analysis. The model that was used to test the hypotheses:

$Y = a + \beta_1 X_1 + e$

Y = Growth of micro enterprises in Thika Sub-County

a = Constant; B_1= Beta coefficient

X_1 = Policy frameworks

e = error term

Table 26: Model Summary

Model	R	R Square	Adjusted R Square	Std. Error of the Estimate
1	.031[a]	.001	-.009	1.68041
a. Predictors: (Constant), Policy Framework				

The findings in Table 26, shows that R-Square value was 0.001, which indicates that the policy framework explain 0.1% of the variation in the Growth of Micro Enterprise in Thika sub county. The remaining 99.9% variations in Growth of the micro enterprises is explained by other factors.

Table 27: ANOVA[a]

Model		Sum of Squares	Df	Mean Square	F	Sig.
1	Regression	.260	1	.260	.092	.762[b]
	Residual	276.730	98	2.824		
	Total	276.990	99			
a. Dependent Variable: Microenterprise Growth						
b. Predictors: (Constant), Policy Framework						

From the Anova Table, the finding shows that the F calculated was 0.92 and sig. value was 0.133. Since F calculated (0.092) was less than F critical (3.938) and sig value (0.762) was greater than 0.05, the overall model was insignificant.

Table 28: Coefficients[a]

Model		Unstandardized Coefficients		Standardized Coefficients	t	Sig.
		B	Std. Error	Beta		
1	(Constant)	3.868	.437		8.852	.000
	Policy Framework	.020	.065	.031	.303	.762
a. Dependent Variable: Microenterprise Growth						

From the findings the regression equation was

$$Y = 3.868 + 0.020X_1$$

The findings shows that holding policy framework constant at zero, the growth of micro enterprises had a coefficient of 3.868. Further, the study established that policy framework would lead to 0.057 insignificant positive change in growth of micro enterprises in Thika Sub County. Hence as per the study findings, the null hypothesis was therefore accepted and it was concluded that there is no relationship between Kiambu County Government policy frameworks and micro enterprises growth in Thika Sub-County.

4.7.3 Hypothesis Three

To test the third hypothesis that "Kiambu County Government incentive programmes do not affect micro enterprises growth in Thika Sub-County", the study conducted a regression analysis.

The model that was used to test the hypotheses:

$$Y = a + \beta_2 X_2 + e$$

Y = Growth of micro enterprises in Thika Sub-County

a = Constant; B_2 = Beta coefficient

X_2 = Incentive programmes

e = error term

Table 29: Model Summary

Model	R	R Square	Adjusted R Square	Std. Error of the Estimate
1	.223[a]	.050	.040	1.63869
a. Predictors: (Constant), Incentive Programmes				

The findings in Table 29, shows that R-Square value was 0.040, which indicates that the incentive programmes explain only 4% of the variation in the Growth of Micro Enterprise in Thika Sub County.

Table 30: ANOVA[a]

Model		Sum of Squares	Df	Mean Square	F	Sig.
1	Regression	13.829	1	13.829	5.150	.025[b]
	Residual	263.161	98	2.685		
	Total	**276.990**	**99**			
a. Dependent Variable: Microenterprise Growth						
b. Predictors: (Constant), Incentive Programmes						

From the Anova Table, the findings shows that the F calculated was 5.150and sig. value was 0.025. This shows that the overall model was significant since F calculated (5.150) was greater than F critical (3.938) and sig value (0.025) was greater than 0.05.

Table 31: Coefficients[a]

Model		Unstandardized Coefficients		Standardized Coefficients	t	Sig.
		B	Std. Error	Beta		
1	(Constant)	5.005	.476		10.510	.000
	Incentive Programmes	-.129	.057	-.223	-2.269	.025
a. Dependent Variable: Microenterprise Growth						

From the findings the regression equation was
$Y = 5.005 - 0.129\, X_2$

The findings shows that holding incentive programmes constant at zero, the growth of micro enterprises had a coefficient of 5.005. Further, the study established that incentive programmes would lead to negative 0.129 change in growth of micro enterprises in Thika Sub County. Thus the study rejected the null hypothesis and concluded that Kiambu County Government incentive programmes have a significant effect on micro enterprises growth in Thika Sub-County.

4.7.4 Hypothesis Four

To test the fourth hypothesis that "Kiambu County Government business skills training programmes do not influence micro enterprises Growth", the study conducted a regression analysis. The model that was used to test the hypotheses:

$$Y = a + \beta_3 X_3 + e$$

Y = Growth of micro enterprises in Thika Sub-County

a = Constant; B_3 = Beta coefficient

X_3 = Business skills

e = error term

Table 32: Model Summary

Model	R	R Square	Adjusted R Square	Std. Error of the Estimate
1	.127[a]	.016	.006	1.66748
a. Predictors: (Constant), Business Skills				

The findings in Table 32, shows that R-Square value was 0.006, which indicates that the business skills explain 0.6% of the variation in the growth of micro enterprise in Thika Sub County.

Table 33: ANOVA[a]

Model		Sum of Squares	Df	Mean Square	F	Sig.
1	Regression	4.501	1	4.501	1.619	.206[b]
	Residual	272.489	98	2.781		
	Total	**276.990**	**99**			
a. Dependent Variable: Microenterprise Growth						
b. Predictors: (Constant), Business Skills						

From the Anova Table, the findings shows that the F calculated was 1.619and sig. value was 0.206. This shows that the overall model was insignificant since F calculated (1.619) was less than F critical (3.938) and sig value (0.206) was greater than 0.05.

Table 34: Coefficients[a]

Model		Unstandardized Coefficients		Standardized Coefficients	t	Sig.
		B	Std. Error	Beta		
1	(Constant)	4.321	.309		13.981	.000
	Business Skills	-.055	.043	-.127	-1.272	.206
a. Dependent Variable: Microenterprise Growth						

From the findings the regression equation was

$Y = 4.321 - 0.055X_3$

The findings shows that holding business skills constant at zero, the growth of micro enterprises had a coefficient of 4.321. Further, the study established that business skills would lead to negative 0.055 change in growth of micro enterprises in Thika Sub County. Therefore the study accepted null hypothesis and concluded that Kiambu County Government business skills training programmes do not influence Micro Enterprises Growth.

4.7.5 Hypothesis Five

To test the fifth hypothesis that "There is no relationship between micro enterprises firm factors and the support initiatives of Kiambu County Government", the study conducted a regression analysis. The model that was used to test the hypotheses:

$Y = a + \beta_4X_4 + e$

   Y = Support initiatives of Kiambu County Government

   a = Constant; B_4 = Beta coefficient

   X_4 = Micro enterprises firm factors

   e = error term

Table 35: Model Summary

Model	R	R Square	Adjusted R Square	Std. Error of the Estimate
1	.019[a]	.000	-.012	7.58247
a. Predictors: (Constant), Firm Factors				
b. Dependent Variable: Support Initiatives				

The findings in Table 35, shows that R-Square value was 0.00, which indicates that micro enterprises firm factors explain 0% of the variation in the Growth of Micro Enterprise in Thika Sub County.

Table 36: ANOVA[a]

Model		Sum of Squares	Df	Mean Square	F	Sig.
1	Regression	1.742	1	1.742	.030	.862[b]
	Residual	4829.479	84	57.494		
	Total	**4831.221**	**85**			
a. Dependent Variable: Support Initiatives						
b. Predictors: (Constant), Firm Factors						

From the Anova Table, the findings shows that the F calculated was 0.030and sig. value was 0.862. This shows that the overall model was insignificant since F calculated (0.030) was less than F critical (3.938) and sig value (0.862) was greater than 0.05.

Table 37: Coefficients[a]

Model		Unstandardized Coefficients		Standardized Coefficients	t	Sig.
		B	Std. Error	Beta		
1	(Constant)	19.678	3.875		5.078	.000
	Firm Factors	.048	.275	.019	.174	.862
a. Dependent Variable: Support Initiatives						

From the findings the regression equation was
$Y = 19.678 + 0.048X_1$

The findings shows that holding firm factors constant at zero, support initiatives of Kiambu County Government had a coefficient of 4.727. Further, the study established that micro enterprises firm factors would lead to 0.048 insignificant change in support initiatives of Kiambu County Government in Thika Sub County. Based on the above findings, the null hypothesis was therefore accepted and it was concluded that there is no relationship between micro enterprises firm factors and the support initiatives of Kiambu County Government.

4.7.6 Hypothesis Six

To test the sixth hypothesis that "Firm factors do not affect the growth of micro enterprises in Thika Sub-County", the study conducted a regression analysis. The model that was used to test the hypotheses:

$$Y = a + \beta_5 X_5 + e$$

Y = Growth of micro enterprises in Thika Sub-County

a = Constant; B_5 = Beta coefficient

X_5 = Firm factors

e = error term

Table 38: Model Summary

Model	R	R Square	Adjusted R Square	Std. Error of the Estimate
1	.254[a]	.065	.054	1.71450
a. Predictors: (Constant), Micro enterprise firm factors				
b. Dependent Variable: Microenterprise Growth				

The findings in Table 38, shows that R-Square value was 0.065, which indicates that the Micro enterprise firm factors explain 5.6% of the variation in the Growth of Micro Enterprise in Thika sub county.

Table 39: ANOVA[a]

Model		Sum of Squares	df	Mean Square	F	Sig.
	Regression	17.082	1	17.082	5.811	.018[b]
1	Residual	246.918	84	2.940		
	Total	264.000	85			
a. Dependent Variable: Microenterprise Growth						
b. Predictors: (Constant), Firm Factors						

From the ANOVA Table, the findings shows that the F calculated was 5.811and sig. value was 0.133. This shows that the overall model was significant since F calculated (5.811) was greater than F critical (3.938) and sig value (0.018) was greater than 0.05.

Table 40: Coefficients[a]

Model		Unstandardized Coefficients		Standardized Coefficients	t	Sig.
		B	Std. Error	Beta		
1	(Constant)	1.935	.876		2.209	.030
	Firm Factors	.150	.062	.254	2.411	.018
a. Dependent Variable: Microenterprise Growth						

From the findings the regression equation was
Y= 1.935+ 0.150X_5

The findings shows that holding micro enterprise firm factors constant at zero, the growth of micro enterprises had a coefficient of 1.935. Further, the study established that micro enterprise firm factors would lead to 0.150 significant change in growth of micro enterprises in Thika Sub County. Therefore the study rejected null hypothesis and concluded that firm factors significantly affects the growth of micro enterprises in Thika Sub-County.

Chapter Five: Summary of Findings, Conclusions and Recommendations

5.0 Summary of Findings

Based on the findings, most of the respondents were female however the study was not gender biased as data was collected from approximately equal number of respondents from both genders. The study also found that most of the respondents were aged between 31 and 40 years and their highest level of education was college. The study also found that most of business in Thika Sub County were Retail Shops which have been existing for a period of 1-3 years. The study also found that these businesses were owned by individuals whose source of their income was from personal savings and family.

The study sought to establish the growth trend of the Micro Enterprise in Thika Sub County and found that in most business in Thika Sub County have had their profitability increasing for the last three years and surprisingly the sales of most businesses have been decreasing over the same period.

The study also sought to determine the influence of policy initiatives on the growth of micro enterprises in Thika Sub County. The study found that Kiambu County Government policy frameworks and micro enterprises growth in Thika Sub-County are not related. The study also found that most of micro enterprises stakeholders in Thika Sub County were not in support of the fact that policy initiatives have led to reduced process of acquiring/ renewal of licenses and less business registration requirements.

The study sought to identify how incentives programmes affect micro enterprises growth in Thika Sub County. The study established that Kiambu County Government incentive programmes have a significant effect on micro enterprises growth in Thika Sub-County. The study also found that most of the micro enterprises stakeholders in Thika Sub County were not aware of influence of availability of roads, water, sewage and sanitation, availability of business loans and on preference in purchases.

The study further sought to assess how business skills affect micro enterprises growth in Thika Sub County. The study established that Kiambu County

Government business skills training programmes do not influence micro enterprises Growth. This was supported by the fact the most of the business stakeholders did not see any need for training in business knowledge and practices on business growth. It was clear that most of the business stakeholders refuted on the importance of training in accounting, financial and marketing skills and training in computer and internet skills.

5.1 Conclusions

The study concluded that Kiambu County Government policy frameworks affects micro enterprises growth. Although the initiatives have not led to reduced process of acquiring/ renewal of licenses and less business registration requirements. The study established that Kiambu County Government incentive programmes have a significant effect on micro enterprises growth in Thika Sub-County.

The study established that Kiambu County Government business skills training programmes do not influence micro enterprises Growth since it clear that training in accounting, financial and marketing skills and training in computer and internet skills might not improve the business growth. The study concluded that there micro enterprises firm factors are not related to support initiatives of Kiambu County Government, however they tend to affect the growth of micro enterprises in Thika Sub-County significantly.

5.2 Recommendations

The Kiambu county government needs to come up with a supportive policy for the establishment of documentation centers and information networks to provide information to microenterprises entrepreneurs since most of the stakeholders of the micro enterprises seemed not to be aware on the importance of various county government initiatives.

There is a need for the county government of Kiambu to come up with strategies to ensure that the owners and the stakeholders of the micro enterprises in Thika Sub County are aware of the need of having business skills and also conduct training for interested stakeholders at a reduced cost or no cost. This will improve their business skills and hence improve the performance of the business.

The Kiambu county government needs to organize workshops for owners of micro enterprises and mobilize the owners on to establish training centers offering entrepreneurial training to small enterprises entrepreneurs and managers. There is need to promote business incubator initiatives so as to promote and support viable innovations which would otherwise be unable to access start-ups.

The government should create policy framework that reinforce marketing of goods and services produced by the youth run business. The youths need to form cooperatives so that they can market their products more effectively and avoid exploitation by middlemen. The government should create public awareness on the youth initiatives and increase platforms for funds e.g. the Uwezo fund and others.

5.3 Suggestions for further research

The main motive of the study was to examine the effect of Kiambu County Government support initiatives on the growth of micro enterprise. The study was limited to Thika Sub-County where the highest number of micro enterprises in Kenya is located but represents an urban setup. A similar study could be carried out focusing on another County with a rural setup and compare the findings. Further studies can be done on different independent variables influencing growth of
micro enterprises in Thika Sub-County.

References

Ackah, J. & Vuvor, J. (2011). *The Challenges faced by Small & Medium Enterprises (SMEs) in obtaining credit in Ghana.* MBA Research Project, Blekinge School of Management, Sweden.

Ainuddin, R.A., Beamish, P.W., Hulland, J. S. & Rouse, M.J. (2007). Resource attributes and firm performance in international joint ventures. *Journal of World Business*, 42(1), 47-60.

Al-Madhoun, M. & Analoui, F. (2003). Managerial skills and SMEs' development in Palestine.*Career Development International*, 8(7), 367-79.

Ardic, O. P., Mylenko, N., & Saltane, V. (2011). Small and medium enterprises: A cross-country analysis with a new data set. *World Bank Policy Research Working Paper Series, No. 5538.*

Aremu, T. & Adeyemi, K. (2015). Survival Strategy for Medium and Small Scale Businesses in Ghana. *Sustainable Development Journal*, 3(5), 202-231.

Aremu, M. A. & Adeyemi, S. L. (2011).Small and medium scale enterprises as a survival strategy for employment generation in Nigeria. *Journal of Sustainable Development*, 4(1), 56-72.

Babbie, E. R. (2010). *The practice of social research.* New York, NY: Wadsworth Badulescu, A. (2011). Start-Up Financing Sources: Does Gender Matter? Some Evidence for EU and Romania. *Annals of the University of Oradea: Economic Science, Romania*, 1, 207-213.

Barney, J. (1991). Firm resources and sustained competitive advantage. *Journal of Management,* 17(1), 99-120.

Barney, J. B. & Mackey, T. B. (2005). Testing Resource-Based Theory: *Research Methodology in Strategy and Management.* 2(2), 1-13.

Belliveau, P. & Sandberg, S. (2009). *Internationalization patterns of Chinese private-owned SMEs: Initial stages of internationalization and cluster as take-off node,* in Larimo, J. & Vissak, T. (ed.) Research on Knowledge, Innovation and Internationalization (Progress in International Business Research, Volume 4) Emerald Group Publishing Limited, pp.89 – 114

Berg, G., Fuchs, M., Ramrattan, R., Totolo, E. & Wagh, S. (2015). *Bank Financing of SMEs in Kenya.* Retrieved from http://fsdkenya.org/wp-content/uploads/2015/10/15-09-11-Bank-Financing-of-SMEs-in-Kenya.pdf [Accessed 3rd March, 2019].

Bonfim, D.B., Daniel, A., Dias, B. & Christine, R.C. (2012). What happens after corporate default? Stylized facts on access to credit. *Journal of Bank Finance*, 36(3), 2007-2025.

Bouazza, A.B., Ardjouman, D. & Abada, O. (2015). Establishing the factors affecting the growth of small and medium-sized enterprises in Algeria. *American International Journal of Social Science*, 4(2),101-121.

Bryman, R. & Bell. E. (2007). *Business Research Methods,* 2th edition. Oxford, Oxford University Press.

Bunyasi, G.N.W. (2015). *Entrepreneurial Factors Influencing the Growth of Small and Medium in Thika District, Kenya.* Retrieved fromwww.http. ir.jkuat.ac.ke/handle/123456789/1717 [Accessed 25th February, 2019].

Chamanski, A. & Waago, S. J. (2003). *Critical Success Factors of New, Technology-Based Firms*, in Kirby, D. A. & Watson, A. (eds.) Small Firms and Economic Development in Developed and Transition Economies, Ashgate, London.

Charbonneau, J. & Menon, H. (2013). *A strategic approach to SME exports growth. The section of Enterprise Competitiveness-* ITC. Taipei-Taiwan: Secretariat, Confederation of Asia-Pacific Chambers of Commerce and Industry.

Chaston, I. & Mangles, T. (2002). *Small Business Marketing Management.*Palgrave, Basingstoke, UK.

Churchill, N. & Lewis, V. (2013). Small Business Growth and the Five Steps. *Harvard Business Review*, 55(1), 32-57.

Cooper, D. & Schindler, P. (2014). *Business Research Methods.* Mc-Graw Hill: New York.

Covin, J. (2014). Entrepreneurship Model Concepts in the Behavioral Firms.*Theory and Practice of Entrepreneurship*, 14(3), 5-21.

Creswell, J. W. (2014). *Research Design: Qualitative, Quantitative and Mixed Methods Approaches* (4th ed.). London: Sage Publications Ltd

Davidsson, P. & Wiklund, J. (1999). *Initial conditions as predictors of new venture performance: A replication and extension of Cooper et al. study.* 44th World Conference of the International Council for Small Business, Naples, 20-23 June.

Delmar, F., Davidsson, P. & Gartner, W. (2003). Arriving at the high-growth firm. *Journal of Business Venturing.*18(2), 189-197.

Draugalis, J. R., Coons, S. J., & Plaza, C. M. (2008). Best practices for survey research reports: a synopsis for authors and reviewers. *American journal of pharmaceutical education*, 72(1), 1-6.

Ewiwile, S. Azu, B. & Owa, F. (2011). Effective financing and management of smallscale businesses in Delta State, Nigeria: a tool for sustainable economic growth.*International Journal of Economic Development Research and Investment*, 2(3), 94-101.

Ezeh, J. A. (1999). *Fundamentals of small business management*. Enugu: Glanic Books.

Fiestas, I. & Sinha, S. (2011). *Constraints to private investment in the poorest developing countries: A review of the literature*. London, UK: Nathan Associates London.

Gachuhi, S.M. (2016). *An evaluation of socio-economic factors influencing the growth of small and medium enterprises in Kenya: A case study of Nairobi County*. Msc Research Project, USIU-Africa.

Gao, Q. (2015). *A Growth Predictive System for Chinese SMEs*. PhD Thesis, University of Warwick, United Kingdom.

Gathogo, G. W. (2011).An analysis of factors affecting the performance of small and medium enterprises in the manufacturing sector in Kenya (case of selected firms in Thika municipality), MBA Research Project, Kenyatta University.

Gichuki, A.J., Njeru, A. & Tirimba, O.I. (2014). Challenges Facing Micro and Small Enterprises in accessing Credit Facilities in Kangemi Harambee Market in Nairobi City County, Kenya. *International Journal of Scientific and Research Publications*, 4(12), 1-25.

Grant, R.M. (1991). The resource-based theory of competitive advantage: implications for strategy formulation. *California Management Review*, 33(3), 114-122.

Grimm, M. & Paffhausen, A. (2014). *Interventions for employment creation in MSMEs in low and middle income countries*. Paper presented at the 8th IZA/World Bank Conference on Employment and Development, August 22-23, 2013 Bonn, Germany.

Hallberg, K. (2014). *Marketed Oriented Strategies for SMEs*. Paper No.5, Vol 3, International Finance Corporation.

Hayford, S. (2012). *The development of small medium enterprises and their impact on the Ghanaian economy*. PhD Thesis, Kwame Nkrumah University of Science and Technology, Kumasi-Ghana.

Hisrich, R. D. (2014). *Entrepreneurship*. New York: McGraw-Hill.

Iota, K. N. & Wehinger, G. (2015). *Unlocking SME finance through market-based debt: securitization, private placements and bonds.* OECD Journal: Financial Market Trends, Vol. 2014/2.

Jocumsen. (2004). How do small business managers make marketing decisions? A model of process. *European Journal of Marketing*, 38(5), 659-674

Johnson, R. B., Onwuegbuzie, A. J. & Turner, L. A. (2007) 'Towards a Definition of Mixed Methods Research'.*Journal of Mixed Methods Research*, 1(2), 112-133.

Kagika A. M. (2016).*Management practices of Small and Medium Enterprises and the challenges in socio-economic sphere: A case study of SMEs in Nairobi City*,MA in Sociology, University of Nairobi, Kenya.

Kamunge, M. S.,Njeru, A. &Tirimba, O. I. (2014). Factors Affecting the Performance of Small and Micro Enterprises in Limuru Town Market of Kiambu County, Kenya. *International Journal of Scientific and Research Publications*, 4 (12), 1-19.

Kang'ethe, F. M. (2018). *Influence of strategic planning on performance of small and medium sized manufacturing firms in Kenya,* PhD Thesis, Jomo Kenyatta University of Agriculture and Technology, Kenya.

Kimuru, P. M. (2018). *Determinants of growth in youth owned micro and small enterprises in Kenya,* PhD Thesis, Jomo Kenyatta University of Agriculture and Technology, Kenya.

Kimuyu. P. (2014). *Micro level Institutions and Revenue Generations: Insights from Kenya's Small Business sector.*Discussion paper, Institute of Policy Analysis and Research: Kenya, No. DP 02/030.

King, K. & McGrath S. (2002). Globalization, Enterprise and Knowledge: Educational Training and Development. *International Review of Education*, 50(1), 74-76.

Kiraithe, P. K. (2015). *Factors that influence loan defaulting by SME owners in Kenya: a study of SMEs within Thika Township of Kiambu County.* MA Research Project, University of Nairobi.

Kombo, D. & Tromp, D.L.A. (2006). *Proposal and thesis writing: An Introduction.* Nairobi: Paulines Publications Africa

Kothari, C.R. (2009). *Research Methods and Techniques.* New Delhi: New Age International Publishers.

Kushnir, K. (2010). *"How do economics define micro, small and medium enterprises (MSMEs)?" Companion Note for the MSME Country Indicators.* Retrieved from: http://www1.ifc.org/wps/wcm/connect/ [Accessed 23rd February, 2019].

Kyalo, K. M. (2016). The extent to which small and medium enterprises support and sustain household needs: The case of Muthurwa market, Nairobi County. Research Project, MA, University of Nairobi.

Lois. S. & Annette, A. (2005). *Support for Growth-oriented Women Entrepreneurs in Uganda.*

International Labour Organization, Geneva, Switzerland.

Luiz, M. (2011). *Factors Affecting SME' Growth.* Prepared for the International Labor Organization (ILO), Geneva, November 2011

Madatta, J. (2011). *The role of entrepreneurial competencies on the success of the SME's in Tanzania: The case study of Ilala and Temeke Municipals.* An Unpublished MSc Thesis Tanzania: University of Tanzania.

Majama. N.S. & Magang, T.I.T. (2017). Strategic Planning in Small and Medium Enterprises (SMEs): A Case Study of Botswana SMEs. *Journal of Management and Strategy*, 8(1), 74-103.

Mashenene, R.G. & Rumanyika, J. (2014). Business constraints and potential growth of small and medium enterprises in Tanzania: A Review. *European Journal of Business and Management*, 6(32), 2-79.

Maragia, I. (2013). *Factors that determine the behavioural aspects of Entrepreneurs in Micro and Small Enterprises in Kenya.* Scangraphics Limited.

Marlow, S. (2013). Empowerment and entrepreneurship: A theoretical framework. *International Small Business Journal.* 33(1), 12-27.

Mead, C. & Liedholm, C. (2013). *The Dynamism of the Developing Countries. MMSEs in Developing Countries.* World Development Group Publishers.

Mira, G. K. & Ogollah, K. (2013). Challenges facing accessibility of credit facilities among Women owned enterprises in Nairobi Central Business District in Kenya. *International Journal of Social Sciences and Entrepreneurship,* 1(7), 377-396.

Mong'are, C.N. (2017). *Factors influencing the growth of small and medium enterprises in Kenya: a case study of Nairobi County.* MBA Research Project, USIU-Africa.

Mugenda, O. &. Mugenda (2012). *Research Methods: Quantitative and Qualitative Approaches.* Nairobi, Acts Press.

Mughan T., Kalantaridis C. &Lloyd-Reason L. (2004). *Competing Effectively in International Markets: Mapping Internationalisation in the Eastern Region.* Proceedings of the 25th Institute for Small Business Affairs (ISBA), National Small Firms Policy and Research Conference, University of Brighton, UK.

Mugo, J. G. (2014). *Financial Innovation Impact on Growth of Micro Financial Institutions in Kenya.* Unpublished MBA Project, University of Nairobi.

Mugodo, B.M. (2014). *Factors affecting growth of small scale real estate companies in Trans-Nzoia County: The case of Setmark Properties.* MSc Research Project, Management University of Africa.

Munyao, C. M. (2018). *A study of the contribution of the executive on the performance of SME's: A study of SME's in Machakos County* , MBA Research Project, United States International University, Kenya.

Mutiria, M. (2017). *Factors influencing small and medium size enterprises access to financing: a case of Kiambu county, Kenya.* MBA Research Project, USIU-Africa.

Mutoko, W.R. & Kapunda, S.M. (2017). Factors influencing small, medium and micro-sized enterprises' borrowing from banks: The case of the Botswana manufacturing sector, *Acta Commercii,* 17(1), 1-9.

Nabutola, J. (2015) *Factors influencing performance of SMEs in Central Business District Bungoma County, Kenya,* Master of Arts Research Project, University of Nairobi, Kenya.

Namusonge, G. (2011). *Determinants of growth oriented small and medium enterprises in Kenya.* Abe Books.

Nganu, M. (2018) *Entrepreneurship training and performance of small and micro enterprises in information communication technology sector in Nairobi City County, Kenya.* PhD Thesis, Kenyatta University.

Nguyen, T.H., Alam, Q. & Prajogo, D. (2008). Developing Small and Medium Enterprises (SMEs) in a Transitional Economy-from Theory to Practice: An Operational Model for Vietnamese SMEs. *Journal of Sustainable Development,* 1(1), 113-121.

Njuguna, S. (2016). *Factors affecting growth of small businesses in Kenya a case of Kariobangi area in Nairobi.* MBA Research Project, United States International University – Africa.

Nyagah, C. N. (2013). *Non-financial constraints hindering growth of SMEs in Kenya: The case of plastic manufacturing companies in industrial area in Nairobi County.* MBA Research Project, Kenyatta University, Kenya.

Nyang'au P. S. (2014). *Role of entrepreneurial leadership in the growth of micro and small enterprises in Thika town, Kenya.* PhD Thesis,Jomo Kenyatta University of Agriculture and Technology. Kenya.

Nyarku, K.M. &Oduro, S. (2017).*Examining the Effect of Corruption and Bureaucracy on*

*SMEs Growth in the Kumasi Metropolis of Ghana.*Retrieved from: https://ideas.repec.org/h/sau/ ueedcc/ 06154-173.html [Accessed 3rd March, 2019].

Obura, O. & Matovu, J. (2011). *Pecking order theory and the financial structure of manufacturing SMEs from Australia's business longitudinal survey.* Retrieved from http://www.webpages.uidaho.edu/~mbolin/okello-obura-matova.htm [Accessed 25th February, 2019].

Orodho, J. (2005). *Elements of Education and Social Research. Research Methods.* Nairobi: Masola.

Ouma, J. O. (2018). *Innovation strategy and performance of small and medium enterprises in Kenya: a case study of Kakamega County*, MBA Research Project, University of Nairobi, Kenya.

Owino, O.A. (2017).*Factors affecting the success of SMEs (a case of tailoring SMEs, Uhuru Market, Nairobi).* MBA Research Project, United States International University- Africa.

Parker, S. C. (2004).*The economics of self-employment and entrepreneurship.* Cambridge, U.K: Cambridge University Press.

Penrose, E. (1959). *The theory of the growth of the firm.* New York: Wiley

Rahman, M.M. (2015). *SMEs and Networking: A Resource-based View Perspective.* Retrieved from: https://www.researchgate.net/publication/279450110[Accessed 20th February, 2019].

Ramadhan, O. A. (2019*). Effect of entrepreneurial competencies on the survival of small and medium enterprises in Kenya.* PhD Thesis, Jomo Kenyatta University of Agriculture and Technology, Kenya.

Rambo, C. M. (2013). Time required to break-even for small and medium enterprises: the Evidence from Kenya. *The International Journal of Marketing Research and Management*, 6(1), 81-94.

Ramsden, N. (2010). *The role of SMEs in employment creation and economic growth: lessons from other countries.* Paper presented at the Nairobi County 12th Annual Symposium, Nairobi County, Kenya.

Rindova, V.P. & Fombrun, C.J. (1999). Constructing competitive advantage: The role of firm-constituent interactions. *Strategic Management Journal,* 20(8), 691-710.

Robertson, M., Collins, A., Medeira, N. & Slatter, J. (2003). Barriers to start-up and their effect on aspirant entrepreneurs. *Education Training*, 5(6), 308-316.

Sanjo, O.M. & Ibrahim, M.O. (2017). The Effect of International Business on SMEs Growth in Nigeria. *Journal of Competitiveness,* 9(3), 67- 80.

Sekaran, U. (2006). *Research Method for Business: A Skill Building Approach.* United Kingdom: John Wiley & Sons, Inc.

Sekaran, U. & Bougie, R. (2013).*Research Methods for Business: A Skill-Building Approach.* 6th Edition, Wiley, New York.

Sitharam, S.&Hoque, M. (2016). Factors affecting theperformance of small and medium enterprises in KwaZulu-Natal, South Africa.*Problems and Perspectives in Management,* 14(2-2), 277-288.

Thuranira, L.K. (2017). *Determinants of performance of micro and small enterprises in Kenya: A case of women enterprises in Meru County, Kenya.* MA Research Project, University of Nairobi, Kenya.

Tomlin, B. (2008). *Clearing hurdles: key reforms to make small businesses more successful.* (Commentary No. 264). Toronto, Canada.

Tundi, C. S. & Tundi, H. (2013). Microcredit, micro enterprising and repayment Myth: the case of micro and small women business entrepreneurs in Tanzania. *American Journal of Business and Management,*2(1), 20-30.

Wanjau, K.L., Gakure, R.W., Magutu, P.O. & Kahiri, J. (2013). The role of quality adoption in growth and management of small & medium enterprises in Kenya.*European Scientific Journal*, 9(7), 312-348.

Wanjohi, A. M. (2010). *Challenges Facing SMEs in Kenya and the Efforts in Progress.*Retrieved from: http://www.kenpro.org/challenges-facing-SMEs-in-Kenya-and-the-efforts-in-progress/[Accessed 3rd March, 2019].

Wangui, G., Njeru, A., Ondabu, I. & Tirimba, L. (2014). Challenges Facing Micro and Small Enterprises in Accessing Credit Facilities in Kangemi Harambee Market in Nairobi City County, Kenya. *International Journal of Scientific and Research Publications,* 4(12), 1-25.

Watson, J. (2007). Modeling the relationship between networking and firm performance. *Journal of Business Venturing,* 22(6), 852-874.

Wernerfelt, B. (1984). A resource-based view of the firm. *Strategic Management Journal* 5(2), 171-180.

William, M. (2006). *Research Methods knowledge base.* Retrieved from www.socialresearchmethods.net/kb/quesresp.php[Accessed 22nd February, 2019].

World Bank (2016). *Doing business in 2016- Measuring regulatory quality and efficiency.*

Retrieved from http:// www.doingbusiness.org/reports/global-reports/doing-business-2016.

Visser, D. (2013). *Constraints facing tourism entrepreneurs in South Africa: Case study of the Gauteng and Mpumalanga provinces,* South Africa. PhD Thesis- University of Pretoria, South Africa.

Yeboah, A.M. (2015). Determinants of SME growth: An empirical perspective of SMEs in the Cape Coast Metropolis, Ghana. *The Journal of Business in Developing Nations*, 14, 23-32.

Appendix 1: Questionnaire

PART A: FIRM FACTORS (Please tick (√) where applicable)

1. **Gender of the Owner:** ☐ Female ☐ Male

2. **Age bracket:** ☐ 18-30 yrs ☐ 31-40yrs ☐ 41-50 yrs ☐ Over 50yrs

3. **In which of the following categories does your business belong?**

Jua Kali Sector ☐ Retail Shops ☐ General Trade ☐

Textile Works ☐ Hospitality Sector ☐

Other category…………………………………………

4. **For how long has the business been in existence?**

1-3 years ☐ 3-6 years ☐ 6-8years ☐ 8-10years ☐ More than 10 years ☐

5. **What is your position in the business?**

☐ Owner ☐ Manager ☐ Employee

Other………………………………………………………………

6. **Sources of capital**

Personal & Family ☐ Others ☐

7. **Please indicate your level of education**

University ☐ College ☐ Secondary ☐ Primary ☐ None ☐

PART B: MICRO ENTERPRISE GROWTH

8. How would you rate your firm's **profitability** performance within the last three years of operation?

Increased ☐

No Change ☐

Decreased ☐

9. How have your firm's **sales** faired in the last three years of operation?

Increased ☐

No Change ☐

Decreased ☐

PART C: COUNTY GOVERNMENT MICRO ENTERPRISE SUPPORT INITIATIVES
INCLUDE THE FOLLOWING:

Please indicate the extent to which you agree with the following statements:

		Strongly Agree	Agree	Neither Agree nor Disagree	Disagree	Strongly Disagree
	Policy Framework					
10.	Reduced process of acquiring/ renewal of licenses					
11.	Less business registration requirements					
	Incentive Programmes					
12.	Availability of Business Loans					
13.	Preference in purchases					
14.	Availability of roads, Water, Sewage and Sanitation					
	Business Skills					
15.	Training in Business Knowledge and Practices					
16.	Training in Accounting, Financial and Marketing Skills					
17.	Training in Computer and Internet Skills